FROM THE 'TROUBLES' TO THE TOWER

By Derek Spence

With Forewords by Gordon Taylor and Wayne Harrison

And including 'How Blackpool got its club back' by Steve Rowland

First published 2019

This paperback edition published 2019

Copyright © 2019 by Derek Spence

No part of this book may be reproduced, stored in a retrieval system, or transmitted by any means without the prior written consent of the author

Pictures courtesy of: Bury Times, Blackpool Gazette,

The Belfast Telegraph and Shutterstock

Front cover design by Alan Hall

ISBN 9781787234277

Self-published using CompletelyNovel.com

This book is dedicated to my loving wife Lyn and my wonderful children Leanna, Matthew, Thomas and Erin. I love you all. Thank you for enriching my life and for all your love and support.

Contents

Chapter 1 1
   Growing up in Belfast – Different from the rest [1952 – 1967]

Chapter 2 [1967-1970] 10
   First steps to becoming a professional footballer - A promising start

Chapter 3 [1970-1973] 21
   Off to England - Oldham Athletic

Chapter 4 [1973-1976] 29
   First team football at last - Bury and promotion success

Chapter 5 [1975 - 1976] 40
   International debut - Fame at last!

Chapter 6 [October 1976] 49
   Bestie and me - Biggest game of my career

Chapter 7 [1976-1977] 60
   Seasiders Part 1 - Blackpool FC

Chapter 8 [1977-1978] 68
   Greece is the word is the word - Olympiacos

Chapter 9 [1978-1980] 82
   Back to Blackpool - Blackpool FC

Chapter 10 [1979-1982] 90
   Into the unknown - Southend United

Chapter 11 [1980] 97
   Other side of the world for 20 minutes - Northern Ireland on tour in Australia

Chapter 12 [1981-1982] 105
  World Cup heartache - Teletext and Billy Bingham
Chapter 13 [1982-1983] 114
  Oriental adventures - Hong Kong Rangers
Chapter 14 [1983-1984] 127
  Back to Bury - The twilight days
Chapter 15 [1984-1987] 132
  What next? - Living without football
Chapter 16 [1987] 140
  Deaths in the family and life gets harder
Chapter 17 [1988-1996] 144
  What happens now? Jobs, I've had a few but not too few to mention
Chapter 18 [1996] 151
  Mauritius - One last footballing fling
Photos...
Chapter 19 [1996] 174
  Back to Bloomfield Road and other adventures - Enjoying life again
Chapter 20 [1997] 180
  A new relationship and a trip to America - Life is good
Chapter 21 [1998] 184
  The 'Troubles' and the 1998 Good Friday Agreement - Peace at last?
Chapter 22 [2002] 193
  A death and a birth
Chapter 23 (2003) 196

Derek gets spliced for a second time - Nuptials

Chapter 24 [2004-2009] 199

Jimmy Nicholl comes calling - But I stay with Blackpool

Chapter 25 (2005) 208

Death of a legend - Bestie - and another daughter

Chapter 26 [2009-2011] 211

The promised land - Blackpool hit the big time

Chapter 27 [2013-2016] 215

Retirement the second time - Derek picks up his bus pass

Chapter 28 219

Fleetwood my second home, and reflections on family and career (May 2019)

Chapter 29 224

Northern Ireland revisited [March 2019]

Chapter 30 235

My all-time club team-mates XI - With a difference

Chapter 31 237

How Blackpool Got Its Club Back - By Steve Rowland

Acknowledgments

I'd like to thank Lyn for coming up with the title of this book and for all her help and support. Without her input and encouragement I would never have finished it which, overall, took over seven years to complete.

Grateful thanks too to Peter Woolstencroft, Paul Cambridge and my Shrimper pal Andrew Leeder for their assistance in putting the book together, Gordon Taylor for his support and foreword contribution, my dear friend Wayne Harrison for providing such a wonderful foreword (almost reduced me to tears - thanks mate), my friend Steve Rowland for the addition of a separate chapter on my beloved Blackpool FC, all the ex-team-mates and managers who helped me have the career I had, the supporters of the clubs I played for (you all have a special place in my heart), my brother Alex and my gorgeous sisters, my four incredible children and my many friends inside and outside of football who encouraged me throughout this project.

FOREWORD BY GORDON TAYLOR

Born in January 1952, Derek was brought up on a housing estate in Belfast and played for Crusaders before coming to England to join Oldham Athletic.

Derek's playing career spanned 15 years playing international football for Northern Ireland with the likes of George Best and playing for Olympiakos in Greece and Hong Kong Rangers. On the domestic front he played at Oldham Athletic, Bury, Southend United and Blackpool (the Seasiders) where he went on to spend over two decades heading up their successful Community Programme. He scored 98 goals in 348 appearances for his clubs and 29 appearances for his country.

Derek was a character in the true sense of the word, and it was through his community work at Blackpool that he really excelled. Everyone he met was inspired by his infectious passion for the role, whether it was youngsters from the tough housing estates to the teachers, authorities and business partners who could make a positive difference for social change.

The PFA were instrumental in setting up the Community Programmes in the mid to late 1980's when the game was at its lowest point. We used former players to bring the clubs and their communities closer together and Derek epitomised that ethos, building bridges with the hardest to reach, bringing communities closer together and instilling a sense of worth and belonging for the club and the region.

He spent over two decades on the Community Scheme and was an inspirational figure in the North-West region. He always went above and beyond and was well thought of and respected by his peers.

The best compliment I could pay to Derek is that the game of football, and the community he served so well, have been changed so significantly for the better and it is because of people like Derek and his tireless appetite to make a positive difference that the Community Programme has become a beacon for others to follow. Great character, great player, and above all a real champion of his community.

Gordon Taylor OBE

FOREWORD BY WAYNE HARRISON

It was 1979 when I joined Blackpool as a player. Everyone made me welcome, especially "Snowball", who I'd never met before, but who ultimately became as close to a brother as I will ever have (I'm an only child).

I had just started to get to know Derek when suddenly he was sold to Southend United. Little did I know then that many years later our paths would cross once more, long after our football playing careers were over.

Usually, central defenders try to scare the life out of centre forwards. But Derek was different, a striker who scared the life out of the defender unfortunate enough to oppose him. He was Jekyll and Hyde. On the field, a rough, tough, skilled competitor who would die for the cause, but off the field the nicest person you will ever meet and one of the funniest and happiest men alive.

Yep, Jekyll and Hyde for sure, but even as Hyde you loved him. As a player, he always gave his all for teammates and supporters alike. Derek had a fantastic career playing 29 times for his country, Northern Ireland, and playing alongside one of the top players of all time, George Best, in an international game against Johan Cruyff and that great Dutch team of the 1970's.

Derek was certainly good enough to play at the top level, but lady luck was never with him. I know Manchester United were very interested in him but, unfortunately for Derek, it didn't happen.

The long blond hair is history and has been replaced by a less eye-catching bald head, but we all get older and whilst

I'm as grey as a husky these days, Snowball still stands out in a crowd, hair or no hair.

By 1996, I had quit playing and, like many other ex-footballers, I was trying to break into coaching. Derek was the Community Development Officer at Blackpool Football Club. We had not stayed in touch when he left the Tangerines as we had only known each other a couple of months by that point but, 16 years later, a chance meeting with Derek would give me the start I was looking for.

You would have thought he'd been in contact with me every day for the past 16 years such was his warmth and friendliness. I'm not sure he was actually looking for an assistant community development officer, but he offered me the job anyway (merely to help me out I'm sure) and so began a true and special friendship that has lasted to this day.

If ever there was a person born to coach young players Derek was the one. He ensured the game was something to be loved, cherished even, and with his big, yet humble, personality, he made a massive impact on every young player who crossed his path.

The pied piper of Hamelin – or Hambleton in Derek's case – we all did our best to match his enthusiasm and motivational qualities. The PFA had an angel in disguise working for them and he epitomised everything that they preached in the football community scheme.

Every year the PFA in each region had a Christmas party and it was the custom for clubs to take turns on an annual basis to stage and organise the event. They were always enjoyable, but Blackpool's was the most entertaining and zany. Such was his success as host that the other clubs voted for Derek to stage and organise the party at Blackpool every year as they were by some distance the most fun occasions.

I remember one year my wife was the manager of a charity shop, so Derek and I bought women's clothing to go to a fancy-dress Christmas party for the community coaches of the north-west clubs. We actually made pretty good-looking ladies, my moustache maybe giving the game away. After the party everyone (except Derek and me of course) changed and we all went out to a night club. Still disguised as ropey looking girls, the glances we got were hilarious, especially when we went to the gents for a pee. I think I had better legs than him though!

Later, I became Academy Director for Blackpool Youth, which wouldn't have happened had Derek not given me my first opportunity. I knew his personality and knowledge would be great for the older teams in the academy so almost immediately I asked him if he would take one of our academy teams. After a little persuasion he said yes - it was such a great move for us as an academy, a successful International player with a love and devotion to Blackpool FC who, as well as being a good coach, could inculcate young players with his positivity and sense of fun.

Very happy days they were working with Derek, both in the community scheme and at the youth academy. We were like two peas in a pod, personality wise.

My wife and family and I eventually left for the USA and we have lived there now for nearly 20 years, with a spell in between living in Dubai. I was and am still coaching for a living.

Let's face it, not a lot of friends make the effort to see you when you are significant distances apart, what with the cost of travelling and the time restraints on taking holidays, but

Derek, his lovely wife Lyn and his smashing children, Thomas and Erin, came to see us in Minnesota several times and our fun just overflowed as it does every time we are together.

After we moved to California, friends who had never shown an interest in visiting us in Minnesota suddenly wanted to look us up. Derek and Lyn, though, were there for us wherever we resided.

Whilst in Dubai I was technical director for a club called Al Ain and we needed a team to play us in a tournament for our Under 16s. I immediately thought of Derek and Blackpool FC. Derek duly came out with a team, worked with the boys and looked after them too of course. I was delighted mainly due to that he and I got the chance to spend a great week together as buddies again. This was surely one of the best weeks of these young footballer's lives. Our club were very hospitable and set them up in the Hilton Hotel and everyone was given five-star treatment. Derek's extrovert personality impressed all who met him, and it was certainly a trip to remember forever for all concerned.

Sadly, my Mum died last year, and Derek and Lyn came to her funeral to pay their respects. They have also travelled up to Cumbria to see my Dad on occasions since then to make sure he's doing okay. That's what true friends are. Despite their busy lives, they always make the effort for us.

Every time we are home from the USA we do our utmost to meet up with Derek and Lyn. The years roll by but nothing changes, we are all still the same people who genuinely love one another and it's always a blast when we are together with plenty of sarcastic banter thrown in for good measure.

What else can I say but thank you Derek for being such a wonderful friend to us in times of trouble and happier times too.

This book is truly a tribute to a great man, on and off the field. A more humble person you could not wish to meet, Derek is always there for everyone he knows.

I cannot speak highly enough about him as a true friend and colleague and wish him great success with his book which I am privileged to have been asked to write the foreword for.

Wayne Harrison

May 2019

Chapter 1
Growing up in Belfast – Different from the rest
[1952 – 1967]

There were three things that set me apart from my friends when I was young. The first and most obvious of these was a great shock of white blond hair: this made me easy to spot, easy to identify and easy to blame for any misdemeanour. It also led to my childhood nickname, "Snowball."

The second feature was my volcanic temper, something for which the Spence menfolk had quite a reputation.

And the third thing was my endless supply of surplus energy. In fact, one of my earliest childhood memories was of the great holes that pockmarked all our chairs and sofas. I would spend hours headbutting anything that wouldn't crack my skull. I would even headbutt the pillow at night. It was the only way I could find to get rid of the excess energy that coursed through my system. These days such behaviour would be diagnosed as ADHD or something similar, but in the Belfast of the 1950's and '60's such terms were unheard of.

I was born on 18 January 1952 in Belfast. When I was a wee boy my family moved to a council house in a mixed community, that is to say, a Catholic and Protestant estate - just off the Whitewell Road. We never had too much trouble from the point of view of sectarianism, although the day we moved into our new home I remember that somebody had taken the trouble to smash all the drainpipes with a hammer, which was a pretty good way of letting us know that somebody would have preferred Catholic neighbours like the previous occupants had been. How did they know we were not a Catholic family? Simple really; anybody from Northern Ireland would know immediately that 'Spence' was a Protestant name.

Number 14 Serpentine Road was home to the Spence family: Daddy, Billy, a joiner with more skill in his tongue than in his tenon saw, and my Mummy who had been born Joan Randall in Ellesmere Port over in England. Mummy spent her whole life in our kitchen. She could rustle up a meal for anybody at any time of the day or night. The doors were always open and people were constantly popping in for a bite to eat, most especially Mrs Craig who lived across the road from us. She would sometimes turn up with her son and daughter in tow, so you can imagine how busy that little kitchen was. Indeed, I have hardly any memories of Mummy anywhere other than the kitchen.

My eldest sister was Isabella, next in line came Maureen, then me. My younger sisters were Doris, Joan and Diane, and then came my little brother, Alex.

Most of us kids were born at home. Daddy, like all the Spence men, was christened William, although everyone knew him as Billy. And continuing the tradition, I am Derek William and my sons are Matthew William and Thomas William.

Billy had been in the RAF during the war. It was whilst doing his patriotic duties that he met my Mummy, who, at that time was working in the big Shell refinery at Ellesmere Port. He was not a big man - about nine stone or thereabouts - but he had big fists and a temper to match. He would regularly get in fights: with us, with the neighbours, and anybody else that pissed him off, with many between him and my Mummy in our tiny kitchen.

He loved boxing and he had given this legalised form of violence a try-out when he was younger, but his temper had persuaded his coaches and other experts to suggest that he find a channel for his aggression somewhere else: anywhere else in fact.

I attended Ballygolden Primary School, which was a two-minute walk from our front door. The head teacher was a man called Mr Moon, who I remember being a lovely bloke. I enjoyed primary school but had a bit of a phobia about arriving late. If I thought there was any chance that assembly had started, on the odd day when I feared I would arrive late, I would run away and spend the rest of the day roaming the fields and open spaces of our neighbourhood. Once in school though, I enjoyed it.

Our home life was normal for a working-class family at that time. We all had our chores to do and mine was lighting the fire. Naturally, as the only boy in a family of girls (until Alex came along) my sisters would wind me up. This would usually result in a chance for me to show off my temper, but by and large things were fine.

The estate was surrounded by hills and open spaces that don't exist now and I used to spend all the hours of daylight exploring and getting into scrapes any time when I wasn't in school. We would go scrumping for apples and would even find rhubarb that had not necessarily been lost. The rhubarb would be handed over to Mummy and I can still remember the smell of it as she cooked it in pies or crumbles.

We lived at the end of our street and next door lived the Bowness family. Their son, Mandal, was a year older than me, and we were the best of friends. About five doors away lived the Nobles: another big family with three sons and three daughters. I am still in touch with one of the sons, Colin, to this very day.

During the summer holidays we would roam the woods that overlooked nearby Cave Hill and would not come home until dark. We all played football together with varying degrees of skill and would kick balls against hedges or anything else that would bounce the ball back to us. This caused more than a few problems with Mandal's daddy, who was a gardener. We knew that if any ball went over his hedge it would be popped, so we would often have to 'acquire' a ball from a nearby garden or else from a school yard. Mr. Bowness' tendency to burst our balls got him into quite a few scraps with my Daddy: encounters which he would inevitably win without much dialogue taking place.

Growing up in the '50's and '60's, the British team to support in Northern Ireland if you were a Protestant was Glasgow Rangers. But although Manchester United were generally regarded as a Catholic club in Northern Irish parlance, many kids from both sides of the religious and political divide supported the Reds, especially after the Munich air disaster and the emergence of Belfast born George Best.

At that time, Liverpool were a Second Division club so very few people followed them, although thousands in Northern Ireland do today.

Always wanting to be different, my team was Spurs. They had won the double in the early '60's and Jimmy Greaves was my hero. Another favourite was Danny Blanchflower, a Northern Ireland international who I was later to play under when he was appointed the national team manager.

I really caught the Spurs bug and even set up a Northern Ireland branch of the Spurs Supporters Club. We once arranged a weekend outing to a Spurs away game at Manchester City, travelling by boat and train. I grew to hold the club in great affection. Even today, I still follow their fortunes although not nearly as avidly as I did back then.

Like most protestant kids, I had a Rangers scarf but I also supported my local club, Crusaders, and loved watching the likes of Mousey Brady and Albert Campbell. I went with Daddy to several Northern Ireland home games at Windsor Park and was enthralled by the atmosphere and sense of occasion.

Despite my growing love of the game, for most of my youth I played no organised football, happy to just play with other kids in the streets whenever an impromptu game sprang up.

On rainy days I would go out and kick a ball about on my own; most of the other kids being too sensible to get a soaking. I would imagine myself to be Jimmy Greaves and would smash the ball into hedges and walls, which I imagined to be the goals of the great stadiums such as White Hart Lane or Old Trafford.

Living conditions by today's standards were hard but normal for the time. We were lucky enough to have an indoor toilet, but the kitchen was tiny. Even so it was the focal point of the house and Mummy used to spend her time there cooking and baking.

On Sundays we would have a big roast dinner accompanied by soup and huge piles of potatoes. Although we were relatively poor, my Daddy demanded proper roast dinners and steaks. He would not eat sausages and other things that he took to be rubbish, so we spent practically all our money on quality food. We didn't have much money left over for sweets or things like that, but bad habits such as dipping bread and marge in sugar ensured that our teeth were just as bad as everybody else's.

When I was ten years old, I joined the Life Boys, which was a junior version of the Boys' Brigade. There was little else for us to do and so the Life Boys and the Presbyterian Church played a strong part in my life. These two organisations were influential in getting us off the streets. There was not much in the way of homework to occupy my time, as I never did any. My Daddy tried his best to help but without much success, and my Mummy was chained to the stove, so homework just passed me by.

Although our family was not very religious, we would occasionally get dressed up and go to church on a Sunday. If Mummy had given us tuppence or threepence to put in the collection, we would put in a halfpenny and spend the rest on sweets.

At the age of ten I suffered an injury that was to have a big effect upon my school life. During a random knife throwing game that would give health and safety officials fits these days, one of my mates managed to throw a knife at my face, just below the left eye. You should have seen the blood. Although it was touch and go for a long time, somehow the doctors managed to save the sight in my left eye. However, with all the trips to the doctors and the hospital, which went on for six months or so, I fell behind in my schooling. Until the accident, I had been in all the top sets, but afterwards found myself languishing in the middle sets, unable or disinclined to catch up on the work I'd missed.

At Dunlambert Secondary School I loved anything practical and was good at metalwork and woodwork, but anything more academic than that was a bit of a waste of time for me. The school didn't really bother to try and teach the less gifted pupils and by the time I got to the last year some of my classmates were so big that they not only frightened me, but they did a pretty good job of intimidating the teachers too.

In that last year at secondary school I had a couple of games of football for the school team. I played in goal. We managed to get into the semi-final of a local cup competition, where I conceded seven goals. The PE teacher gently suggested that I might want to try playing in another position, so from then on, I was an outfield player, playing either on the wing or as a striker.

Once I changed position my fortunes were transformed. In an important game against Orange Field School, I scored the equaliser, just moments before the game was abandoned due to the extreme cold of the day. That performance got me noticed and I was then asked to play for a club called Cairn Lodge. To get to the club I had to catch two buses, one of which went down the famous, some might say notorious, Shankhill Road.

The manager of Cairn Lodge was a bloke by the name of Artie MacFarland, an ex-policeman, and it was his faith in my abilities that made the difference. Artie was also of the opinion that my future did not lie between the sticks and he encouraged me to play up front in a traditional centre forward role. With my physical strength and boundless energy, I caused mayhem among any defenders unlucky enough to discover they were marking me.

One of the little training exercises we did at Cairn Lodge was to play a `one against one' game in which the only players were the goalie and an outfield player. We used hard backed wooden chairs as the goals, so to score a goal between posts just a foot or so apart was a great way to develop shooting skills.

Cairn Lodge played in a strip of red, white and blue, so you can imagine which side of the sectarian divide they represented.

The area around the club was no place for Catholics. At the time, although I was aware of tensions between the divided communities, I was never the object of any hostility based on my religion. Fortunately, the neighbourhood we lived in was home to Catholics and Protestants alike. Indeed, I can recall as a kid playing football in the streets with Bobby Sands who later became a notorious IRA figure and died in the Maze Prison in 1981 after leading a hunger strike, during which he was elected as MP for the constituency of Fermanagh and South Tyrone.

Indeed, you often didn't know until you'd become friends with people what religion they were. I even recall Catholic friends joining in with the singing of loyalist songs during the marching season when the flute bands, which I loved, strode through the streets. To us back then, they were just catchy tunes and we hummed or sang along without really knowing what the songs portrayed.

But at the end of the '60's, things started to change for the worse and I remember when one of my mates and I wandered into a Catholic part of the city by mistake we were chased out by a gang of lads. I was lucky enough to get away, but the lads caught my mate and kicked seven bells out of him. Many years later, my younger brother Alex was unlucky enough to witness a shooting when two gunmen killed a police officer right in front of him at a Crusaders football match.

The World Cup in 1966 was a huge inspiration for me and after that I knew I wanted to be a professional footballer. Frankly, I wanted a life that would get me away from Belfast. Even though the 'Troubles' had not yet reached their nadir, life was hard and it was obvious that the tension between the respective communities was eventually going to explode into a form of brutal civil war.

As 1969 ended and 1970 began, things were starting to get heated between the various political and religious factions. British soldiers appeared on the streets ('Operation Banner') and occasionally we would hear the crack of rifle fire from snipers.

It was at Cairn Lodge that I started to take my football seriously. Whilst my mates would go out for a drink on Friday nights, I would stay in. On the odd occasion when I did go out, I would always come back home on the last bus. I never really fell into the drinking culture that was so prevalent then, although I remember one time I must have broken my rule by getting drunk on scrumpy. Daddy was none too pleased when he opened the door to see me paralytic. He gave me a right-hander to show me the error of my ways. To this day I still can't stand cider.

Chapter 2 [1967-1970]
First steps to becoming a professional footballer - A promising start

Cairn Lodge provided me with the ideal platform from which to showcase my skills and it wasn't long before I started to get noticed. The only cloud on the horizon was the fact that, having now left school aged 15, I had yet to find a form of employment which satisfied me.

My first full-time job was as a messenger boy, delivering parcels for the Exide Battery Company on Dublin Road. I used to ride around Belfast on one of those old fashioned, sit up and beg bikes with a big basket on the front. I doubt they would have hired me if they had known of my obsession with torches and batteries and I soon built up quite a store of these, which somehow managed to find their way into my possession.

The company also had eyes on me becoming an apprentice auto electrician with them, but a couple of things got in the way.

The first obstacle was that I was never going to be good enough on the academic front to do such an apprenticeship.

The second obstacle was a bit more radical. A big lad called Tommy from the Ardoyne was the van driver and I was always mithering him to let me drive the van. "You're not driving that van, because you don't know how to fucking drive" was his not unreasonable point of view. But I must have nagged him so much that one day he agreed to let me reverse the van out of the yard.

The consequences of my unofficial stint as a van driver were predictably dire. As Tommy directed me out of the yard, I got the pedals mixed up and when he called out for me to stop, I instead slammed my foot on to the accelerator and managed to crash into, not one, not two but three cars! It just so happened that one of these cars was a nice new Rover, the pride and joy of the director of the company. Naturally, as I had no licence, I was uninsured.

I thought the best thing to do was to get the 'hell out of there. Immediately!

I never said anything to my parents, but my short-lived secret was revealed when there was a knock at our door later that evening and who should be standing there but the company director. Once inside he went on to explain what I had done and started to talk about me making reparations for the damage I had caused, which must have run into several hundred pounds.

Daddy just laughed and said, "have you had a good fucking look around?" This frank discourse rapidly convinced the director that he had two chances of getting the money back: slim and fuck all. And slim had just left town.

When Daddy had finished reminding the boss that the final responsibility lay firmly with Tommy, who had been foolish enough to allow me to get behind the wheel of the van, it became clear the Spence family was not going to be out of pocket.

They didn't even sack me. It's a wonder I didn't get a pay rise. Thinking about it, Daddy was born at least 50 years before his time. If he'd been around today, he would have made a cracking football agent.

Ultimately, I knew I was never going to be an auto electrician and so, three months later, I handed in my notice.

I ended up on an apprentice scheme, but this time with the aim of becoming a joiner. This was at a government run establishment called Feldenn House. I had always enjoyed working with wood and found the practical side of things to be really satisfying; making dovetail joints and the like. Some of my work was so good that it was displayed on the walls and I still have the toolbox I made with my own fair hands.

I found myself working with a lad called Chris McConnell. During our dinner breaks we would have knockabout games of football with the brickies, plumbers and the like. The only problem with Chris was that he was every bit as competitive as I was and somehow or other we always seemed to end up on opposite sides. A clash was bound to happen and one day it did. We ended up in a bit of a fist fight, probably over something utterly trivial, but whatever it was it seriously soured our relationship. Thereafter things were a bit tense between us, which was a bit problematic given that for much of the time at work we were sharing the same bench.

Daddy had often given me a piece of what I took to be good advice: "Always get your retaliation in first!" The problem was that I took it too literally and my temper always seemed to be getting me in lumber.

Chris was a good footballer and played for Crusaders, one of the semi-professional teams in Northern Ireland. They continue to go strong today and they still have the same nickname - the Hatchetmen. You can guess from this that finesse was not their strong point, so it seemed appropriate that somebody with a temper like mine should join the team and that is what I did. They had been scouting me for quite a while and knew what I was about. I started off in the reserves and after scoring a few goals, subsequently made my way in to the first team.

Daddy used to come and watch me when I was at Crusaders, and at one game he took exception to a particularly enthusiastic challenge that saw me laid out on the pitch. So incensed was he that he tried to invade the pitch to belt the living daylights out of my assailant. Luckily for both parties, his progress was hampered by the spiked iron railings that surrounded the pitch. Daddy may well have lost his temper, but he came pretty close to losing something a lot dearer to him as the crotch of his trousers snagged on the spikes. The lad who felled me that day will never know how lucky he was. I was taken off as a result of the challenge and so there were two members of the Spence clan injured that day.

Wherever I went my temper went with me. There was an incident when I was playing for Crusaders Reserves that was typical of me. I was playing with a lad called Lawrence Graham, who had been a good mate of mine when we were at school together. We played an away game at Bangor and we lost.

After the match there was a big argument in the dressing rooms and Lawrence, who was on my side don't forget, said something that I took exception to, insinuating that the defeat had been my fault. So naturally, I squared up to him and it all kicked-off. Bangor took a pretty dim view of away teams fighting amongst themselves in their facilities and sent a letter of complaint to Crusaders. Not that it made the slightest bit of difference to me.

It is odd how you mellow over the years. Nowadays, although I still get quite heated when something or someone irritates me, I rarely really lose it like I did as a youngster.

Despite my hot head, I eventually got picked for the Crusaders first team. My old pair of boots were getting well past their sell-by-date, and I couldn't help but notice that somebody had left a pair of boots behind. Given that, at home, there was never any money to spend on luxuries like football boots, I took it upon myself to 'borrow' these apparently ownerless boots.

It turned out that they belonged to a lad called Ivan Park, who had just left Crusaders to play for a League of Ireland team, down in the Republic. Thirty odd years later I ran into a mate of his in a pub in Dublin and managed to get hold of Ivan on the phone. It was a case of better late than never, as I confessed to the theft of his boots. He didn't appear too bothered and seemed pleased that it was his old boots that had started me off on my professional career.

The Crusaders first team represented quite a step up in class. By this time, 1969, I was still a gangly 17 and very, very raw.

The manager was a bloke by the name of Sammy Todd but he must have seen something in me and I managed to get a handful of first team games under my belt.

One of my more memorable appearances was against Linfield, a team with a massive following, who went on to play Manchester City the following year at Maine Road in the European Cup Winners Cup.

The Crusaders had some legends of Irish football in their team at that time; men like Albert Campbell, Norman Pavis and Mousey Brady. These were players I had idolised as a kid.

After being at Crusaders for a while I got a call up for the Northern Ireland youth team. The youth set up was entirely amateur, as there was no recognised professional football played in Northern Ireland at the time. And any football that was played was always on a Saturday. Both religious groups frowned on Sunday football. Sunday was a day of rest and in many ways it was nice to have a day without the shops being open - a day when family came first (after the morning service at least). In many ways I think that the values of those old times were a lot better than those of today, with our modern obsession with mobile phones and a culture of being able to get anything at any time of the day or night.

My first match for the Northern Ireland youth team was in 1970 against England at Coleraine, about an hour's drive away from Belfast. I went on the team coach, but my Daddy and his mate, Harry Branagh, drove there in daddy's old Ford Consul.

Daddy was always on the last minute for everything and was one of those blokes who could never find his car keys. Wherever they were, and however they got there, it was never his fault of course!

Anyway, they must have set off late and were probably speeding. I don't know the exact details, but I do know that they ended up in a ditch. They could have been killed but, loyal to the end, they hitched a lift to the game and still managed to see my debut.

They were to be rewarded for their tenacity. We beat England and I managed to score the winner. Not a bad start.

The next game in the Home Countries Youth Championship was at home against Wales, which saw another win for Northern Ireland. I was on target again, so with two goals in two games my confidence was sky high.

We went into the last game against Scotland unbeaten. The last match was at Clydebank. We only had to get a draw to win the championship so plenty was at stake and for the first time I experienced pre-match nerves.

Rumour had it that a Rangers scout was in the crowd and a story went around that I was the object of his interest. My goal-scoring record ensured that I was in the starting line-up. I scored twice in the first half and we were leading 2-0 at half-time.

Daddy was again in the crowd and I can only imagine how proud he must have felt because, typically of men in those days, he said very little to me personally afterwards. That said, I always knew instinctively that he took great pride in my achievements. You can sense these things even without words being exchanged.

In the Scotland team that day was a young fella by the name of Derek Parlane. Rudely, Parlane scored three times in a ten-minute period and suddenly we were losing 3-2 and our dreams of glory were fading fast. With ten minutes to go, up popped a wee fella by the name of Fergie McKelvey who equalised. All we had to do was hold on for the draw and the championship was ours. It was like the Alamo for those last ten minutes, but we managed to hang on and I'd won my first trophy as a footballer.

Sadly, for me at least, it was Parlane who got a contract with Rangers, going on to become a firm Ibrox favourite and ending his top-class career in England with the likes of Leeds United and Manchester City.

That was, to the best of my knowledge, the only time that Northern Ireland had ever won the Home Championship. They certainly have not managed to repeat the feat in the intervening years, and we did it with a tiny pool of players.

As is invariably the case, only two of that squad went on to have significant professional careers: Jim Platt (long-time goalkeeper at Middlesbrough), and me! The rest of my teammates did however enjoy distinguished semi-professional careers in Ireland with people like Paul Kirk, Roy McDonald and Alan Frazer being some of the names that stand out in my memory.

If the football was going well, the working side of my life was not running as smoothly. After a year at Feldenn House, I left the training centre to take up a role with F. B. McKee, a massive civil engineering company who had started to work on a new Post Office on the Falls Road. Despite my part in its creation, the Post Office is still there to this very day.

I was indentured to them for four years and went from making delicate dovetailed joints to being a hairy-arsed shuttering joiner whose most delicate tools were a dirty great hammer and a six-inch nail. I had wanted to be a cabinet maker, but the fates conspired to thwart this ambition.

In my new job, I went to work every morning on a little Honda 50 moped and naturally my mates would play pranks on me, like letting my tyres down, hiding the bike, or switching off the petrol valve so I couldn't start the bloody thing.

One of the most annoying things about the new job was that, even in the middle of winter, we apprentices were not allowed to go into the brew room for a cup of tea and warm up, as the time-served tradesmen would not let the young indentured lads into the brew cabin. So, instead I used to go and find a little cubby hole, line it with cardboard and get my head down for a few hours. Needless to say, this wilful act of industrial truancy made young Derek a bit difficult to locate when it came to allocating him jobs.

How I survived my time on the building sites, Lord alone knows. My survival was certainly not down to the health and safety regulations, because as far as I could tell, there were none. A parting of the ways was inevitable, so I went to see my boss to hand in my notice.

He was somewhat taken aback by this and even more so when I told him that I was going to be a professional footballer.

When he enquired which club I was going to play for, I replied; "Stockport County!" Fuck knows why I mentioned them as to the best of my knowledge they had never heard of me!

I got home on Friday night and confessed to Mummy that I had jacked in the joinery. She confined herself to the one question that she knew was at the heart of the matter: "Have you told Daddy?"

When I told Daddy, he was none too pleased. His reaction was to kick me up the arse and tell me that I had better get a job quickly, as the Spence household had no room for freeloaders. Remember that this was at a time when tensions between the Protestant and Catholic communities were worsening on a daily basis and finding work was now more difficult than ever.

In order to escape the wrath of Daddy, I began immediately to look for another job. Somehow or other I got an interview with a bloke with the unlikely name of Mr Pope! I was to go and see him at a little joinery company on the Shankhill Road, the heart of Protestant Belfast. Brave man.

I must have impressed Mr. Pope because, without further ado, he took me on. My job was to do general repair work on little terraced houses. I had to work on properties in both the Protestant and Catholic areas, and so it was, in its own way, quite a precarious job.

Bear in mind that I was, in truth, just a second-year apprentice, but in my new role I was somehow elevated to the rank of a time-served tradesman. And not only that, I had my own labourer; a local lad who used to wheel all our gear about on a handcart. Having a van of my own would have represented the sum of all my ambitions at that time, but as it was, I had to settle for the handcart.

After six months or so of working on both the Shankhill and Falls roads with my faithful labourer, I thought the best thing for it was to throw my lot in with Daddy, who worked for a refrigeration company called J. Oliver Leech that had been set up by two English blokes. Their offices and yard were right next to Windsor Park, where the Northern Ireland football team played its home games.

We used to travel around Belfast and put insulation into cold stores for large butchers and the like. This was a pretty cushy number, especially when Daddy would clock me in so I could get the overtime whilst I was off playing football. I loved that job. We used to drive around in a little Morris Minor van: Daddy, another fella, and me. There was only supposed to be room for two passengers and I always ended up sitting on top of the overheated gearbox. I was convinced that it was this seating arrangement that gave me a nasty case of the piles.

The other thing that was not so great was that both Daddy and the other bloke smoked incessantly. They would light up the scrag-ends of scrounged and saved cigarette butts and the van would fill up with smoke. I would always be trying to hang my head out of the window to get a breath of fresh air. I had always disliked smoking but my mild loathing soon turned to hatred whilst employed in that job.

Apart from the piles and the smoking, though, these were good times. I was earning £25 or £30 a week, which was good money, but although I was happy enough, I knew it was never going to last. I wanted to play football. And I wanted to leave Belfast and the 'Troubles' behind me.

Chapter 3 [1970-1973]
Off to England - Oldham Athletic

In the early part of 1970 and in the wake of my performances for the Northern Ireland youth team, I got the chance of a trial at Birmingham City who were a First Division club at the time, equivalent now to the Premier League. I had two weeks there, played in several trial games and scored a few goals. It was while I was there that I first met a bloke called Stevie Phillips, who I was later to play with at Southend United. Stevie went on to become a prolific striker in the lower leagues.

Initially, Birmingham wanted to sign me, and it looked like I was going to join them for pre-season training in the July. However, that fell through when they suddenly appointed a new manager in Freddie Goodwin who wanted nothing to do with any deals made by his predecessor, so, agonisingly it was back home to Northern Ireland for me.

Naturally I was devastated, but all was not lost. Crusaders had a contact at Oldham Athletic. The Latics were in the old fourth division at that time but they were a club with history and big ideas and would seal promotion to Division Three during my first season at the club (1970/71).

Anyway, to cut a long story short, scout Sammy McEown arranged for me to go and have a trial with Oldham during the summer. A goalie called Dennis Matthews, who also played for Crusaders, came over with me and the club put us up in digs in Oldham. I remember the weather was really hot, which was unusual, because even in summer Oldham is one of the coldest places in England.

The digs we were in had an outside toilet. This represented a major come down for me, as even our Belfast council house had an inside loo.

Oldham's ground, Boundary Park, is very different now to the ground I knew during my time with the club. Back then we called it 'Sheepfoot Lane' in tribute to a nearby street which, comparable to all the others in that area, was cobbled like those that feature at the beginning of Coronation Street. It made me think of that old joke... a bomb went off and did £5,000 worth of improvements! Not that with my Ulster roots I would have attempted that joke at the time.

Oldham played in a strip which featured blue shirts and, of all things, orange socks. Despite my Protestantism, the combination was not an appealing one, and later they changed to white socks, which, for some reason, I always loved. I think they reminded me of Real Madrid although nothing else about Oldham Athletic did.

Pre-season training was very physical with lots of lads out to make a name for themselves. I played in a few games, did well and on the strength of my performances they asked me to stay on for another couple of weeks. Dennis must have impressed them as well, as he got the same offer.

After this second two-week trial they offered me professional terms but, sadly, let Dennis Matthews go. I was delighted with their offer and somewhat surprised, as I had been up against people who had served out their apprenticeships at the club. The fact that I relished the physical side of the game was probably the deciding factor.

As, of course, there were no agents in those days and I wanted a bit of moral support, Daddy came over from Belfast for the signing of the contract. Naturally, this ceremony took place in a pub, The Grapes.

The Club Secretary, Bernard Halford, who went on to perform the same role for many years at Manchester City, was Oldham's representative alongside manager Jimmy Frizzell and suddenly, there I was, Derek William Spence, a pro footballer.

I initially signed a one-year contract on 5 September 1970 until 30 June 1971. In June of each of the following two years I was offered one-year renewals.

They offered me £17 a week, plus £5 a week if I played for the first team, which represented quite a drop in wages from the money I had been earning as a chippie, but Daddy saw it for the opportunity it was: a chance for me to get out of Belfast and make my living doing the thing I loved. It was a no-brainer. During my tenure at Oldham, my wages went from £17 a week to the dizzy heights of £21. Harry Kane eat your heart out.

The bonuses I was on make interesting reading. During that first season when, at its conclusion, Oldham won promotion to the Third Division, I was on the following incentives:

- Top four places in Fourth Division: £8 per point (£9 if playing away);
- Places five to eight: £6 per point (£7 if playing away);
- Places nine to 12: £3 per point (£4 if playing away)
- Place 13 to 24: £2 per point (£3 if playing away).

In addition, if we finished in the top four at the end of the season, a £3,000 pot was to be shared amongst the players and divided on the number of appearances per player.

The reserve team bonuses were £2 for a win and £1 for a draw. It was almost exclusively those which applied to me as I saw precious little first team action.

Oddly, unlike most other North West league clubs, Oldham's Reserve team didn't play in the Central League. Unfortunately for me, they played in the Cheshire League, which was home to some pretty tough old pros who had had their own careers and were now on the way to footballing retirement.

There were some formidable teams in that league like Burscough, Nantwich and Northwich Victoria. Between the old-timers, who were hell-bent on maiming somebody, and the youngsters equally determined to kick their way to stardom, the Cheshire League proved to be quite a baptism of fire. You knew that if you got the ball and decided to hold it up, somebody was going to come in from behind and clatter you. And if you didn't return the favour with interest, you would never have survived. Any weakness was pounced on by the cloggers. If you had turned the other cheek, some bugger would have tried to kick it off your face.

In spite of the hazards, it turned out to be a very good grounding for my subsequent professional career and probably worked to my advantage. It toughened me up and I rapidly learned all the tricks of the trade. Had I played in the more virtuous Central League I doubt that I'd have been as well prepared for first team football once that opportunity finally presented itself.

Problem was, the opportunity to play first team football was as far away as ever. I played for Oldham reserves for almost three seasons and yet despite being a prolific goal scorer at that level I only made six first team appearances. Normally, your first team debut in professional football is something you look back on with pride, but I can barely remember it. I think it was against Chesterfield. I know I didn't score, and I probably had an ordinary game because, as I say, I can't recall any details.

But, my un-memorable debut aside, there was a reason for my lack of progress that was totally unrelated to my impressive performances. Although I didn't know it at the time, there was a clause in my contract that said if I played a certain amount of games in the first team (and guess what, the magic number was seven!) then Oldham had to pay a bonus to Crusaders of £2,000. No wonder I wasn't getting anywhere. The tight buggers were too stingy to pay the bonus. I was scoring 20 goals a season in the stiffs yet rarely getting a sniff of first team action. And all the while my colleague Ian Robbins was getting lots of exposure, coming off the bench to make substitute appearances.

I knew nothing of this bonus clause and assumed that the coach, Walter Joyce, had it in for me. This turned out not to be the case. The truth of the matter is that I owe a lot to Walter - I could never have become the player I eventually became without his encouragement. He took the time to coach and inspire us youngsters and many of us went on to enjoy long professional careers.

Walter was a great coach and went on to take up the same role at Manchester United. Eventually, we lost touch but I was lucky enough to bump into him again shortly before his death and tell him how invaluable his coaching and encouragement had been to me. I'm pleased to see that his son, Warren, is still in the game. After playing for Bolton Wanderers, Preston North End, Plymouth Argyle, Burnley and Hull City, he had a brief spell managing Hull City before taking a long-term post coaching Manchester United's reserve side.

After his sacking by Wigan Athletic during season 2016/17, Warren was appointed manager of Melbourne City on the recommendation of former England manager, Roy Hodgson, but left their employ after two disappointing seasons.

The first full football season of the 1970's was a turning point in the history of the English game, for it was at this point that companies first started sponsoring club competitions. With ticket sales dwindling and hooliganism rising, it seemed football in England was going through a crisis of sorts, but that didn't stop corporate entities queueing up to put their name to the various competitions.

One such sponsorship deal was the Ford Sporting League - not a competition in the traditional sense, simply an innovative, one-off attempt at promoting and encouraging positive aspects of the game. The concept was simple enough: every time one of the 92 Football League clubs scored a goal during the 1970/71 season, they'd receive one point. When they scored away from home, they'd score two points. If a player received a yellow card, however, they'd be deducted five points, while a red card came with a ten-point penalty.

Season 1970/71 was a very good year for Oldham Athletic. They not only secured promotion to the Third Division, but also won the Ford Sporting League and the money from that meant that they could build a new stand. Oh, and the savings from not paying Crusaders of course! And perhaps if I had been playing regular first team football my frequent bookings might have impaired their chances too.

The Latics had a lad who played up front for them called Jim Fryatt. He was the best header of a ball I had ever seen and I used to spend hours alone on the training ground trying to copy him. Bobby Collins was also a player I admired enormously, and I was desperate to be playing alongside these blokes regularly and not just in training.

Oldham went up in third place and, as I signed my second contract in June 1971, I still hoped I'd become a first team fixture the following campaign.

I didn't of course and although the club enjoyed a solid debut season in Division Three it all pretty much passed me by as I continued my sojourn of the Cheshire League grounds in the stiffs.

I was still in digs at the time, still enduring the outside toilet, so spending time at the training ground was actually preferable to being at home.

On a more positive front, one nice little perk of being a footballer was that I finally discovered women. I'd left Northern Ireland as green as grass. I knew nothing about girls, had never had anything remotely akin to a girlfriend and was in blissful ignorance about the birds and the bees and who did what to whom and why.

Although I'm sure my natural good looks, aligned to my eye-catching blonde locks, were enough on their own to attract English women, my status as a professional footballer, however humble my achievements thus far, didn't do me any harm in the pulling stakes either.

During my last season at Oldham (1972/73), the first team just missed out on promotion by finishing fourth in Division Three. It was a good side with the likes of Keith Hicks, Harry Dowd, Steve Hoolickin, Dave Shaw, Bobby Collins and Johnny Morrissey featuring prominently, but I couldn't help feeling that if I'd been given a run in the side I'd have given them that extra edge to finish in the top two.

Oldham finally got promoted to Division Two at the end of the 1973/74 season as champions, but by early 1973 it was crystal clear that if I wanted regular first team football I was going to have to move and I'd long departed the Latics by the time that championship winning season got underway.

Chapter 4 [1973-1976]

First team football at last - Bury and promotion success

Fourth division Bury were keen to have me as a loan player, so I thought I would go and have a chat with them. This would be February 1973.

During negotiations with Bury I would drive over in my little Mini Cooper and try to represent myself as best I could. Their manager at the time was Allan Brown and he must have had a bit of a soft spot for me, as he bought me twice: once for Bury and later when he was manager at Blackpool.

Allan was a former Scottish international who had been a centre forward very much in my own style - all hustle and bustle. Allan offered me a loan deal until the end of the season, and I was just about to accept, when the Bury chairman Billy Allen upped the ante and offered me a full-time professional contract on £35 a week. There was no way I was going to miss a deal like that.

I thought that maybe Oldham had been in the dark about all this, but when I went back to have a word with the chairman, John Lowe, about my plans he asked, "Well, Derek, have you made your decision?" Before I had time to answer, he did the job for me, saying, "We'll be sad to see you go!"

The truth of the matter was that they were delighted to see me leave. Not only did they get £2,500 for me, but this new deal meant they would not have to pay Crusaders their £2,000. It would be easy to allow myself to be bitter about spending so much time playing reserve team football, but on reflection, those three years at Oldham stood me in good stead. They gave me the time to mature as a player, and by the time I was 21 I was ready to be a first team player.

I signed my first contract with Bury on 14 February 1973 in a 16-month deal until June 1974. So, four more months security than I was used to. The big time.

And if I played for the first team I got an extra fiver. I was also due £10 if we played against a second division side in the League and FA Cup competitions, with that figure rising to a monumental £15 if we drew a top-flight club.

Bury had just sold their most high-profile player, Terry McDermott, to Newcastle United and I remember that the local paper did a feature on his departure and my arrival. The headlines were along the lines of; "Goodbye, Terry: Hello, Derek." Hardly the stuff of which Pulitzer Prizes are made, but at least I felt welcome. Terry, of course, went on to play for his boyhood idols Liverpool, winning every honour in the game, and was assistant manager to Kevin Keegan at Newcastle United during the 'I'd love it if we beat them' era.

Bury were mid-table in the fourth division at that time and one of the things they might have been a bit worried about in their new striker was his weight. I weighed about ten and a half stone at the time. In order to bulk me up they told me to drink a couple of bottles of J. W. Lees' stout every day. I used to drink it in my digs and at first thought it was foul, but in the end I developed quite a taste for stout and I still like Guinness to this day.

I put on about half a stone with this cutting-edge nutritional regime and then stayed at 11 stone throughout my playing career. I don't weigh that much more today.

I never suffered any really serious injury during my playing career and never broke any bones. A doctor who examined me once told me that I had very dense, hard bones and that was why I was able to withstand all those challenges from defenders out to make a name for themselves. So maybe the stout was beneficial after all.

The dressing room at Bury was absolutely brilliant: a great bunch of lads who really got on and played for each other. We played attractive, attacking football and we were getting home gates of 10,000: not bad for a fourth division side. The craic and the camaraderie were terrific, especially when we travelled to away games.

At the various hotels we stayed in, me and a lad called Steve Hoolickin, who had also moved from Oldham to Gigg Lane, would make it our mission to mess up everybody's rooms. Sometimes, things went a bit too far and when Steve decided to hold his stag night at the supporters' club bar, somehow or other it all kicked off and there was a mass brawl which ended up with the players being banned from their own supporters' club. Imagine what a scandal the press and social media would make of that today! Not for nothing did some people rename him Steve Hooligan rather than Hoolickin.

Ironically, after finishing his playing career, Steve became a publican, so he probably already knew how to bar undesirables without attending any management training courses.

Bury played an enterprising 4-2-4 formation and I played about 10 first team games in this system up until the end of that first season. I remember playing against Hereford United who were promoted as the 1972/73 fourth division champions. We played them at Gigg Lane and beat them 2-0. I scored both goals, one a real bullet of a header and the other one of all things was an overhead kick. From that moment I never looked back, I was leading goal-scorer and I was very popular with the fans, but for some reason I never got voted Player of the Year. I'm not bitter though. Honest.

Bury finished a modest 12th, ten points off a promotion place, but the vibes were great, and I just knew that I was going to be very happy at the club.

Ahead of the 1973/74 season, we signed Peter Swan, who had previously been banned from the game for eight years for his part in a match fixing and betting scandal. He was a class player though and had played 19 times for England. He was about 34 at the time and had, like Muhammad Ali, seen his best years stripped away from him.

We also had Jimmy Nicholson, a Northern Ireland international, a Belfast boy like me, and a former Busby Babe who came to Bury to see out the tail end of his career after giving Huddersfield Town long and distinguished service.

We had a great keeper too, by the name of John Forest and so all in all we had a good team.

In August I was rewarded for my contribution the previous season with an amended contract up to June 1974 and a wage increase of £2.40 per week. I was also given a £2 per week travelling allowance and a signing on fee of £250 to be paid in three instalments.

Bury gelled superbly as a team that year and I was really enjoying my football. I loved Gigg Lane and the backing of their fantastic fans always spurred me on. Despite the humble settings and status, I felt like I was living the dream.

I remember scoring a goal against Barnsley at Gigg Lane, which I am reliably informed is still regarded as one of the best goals ever seen at the ground. I picked the ball up at the corner flag, beat four players and whacked it into the top corner of the net. I was always a very instinctive sort of player - always ready to try something unusual.

These days, with the game so tactical and players micro-managed from the technical area by demented managers who seemingly feel they have to talk their multi-million pound players through every second of the 90 minutes, I often wonder just how I would have fitted in to the modern game. I just played on instinct and was at my best when given the freedom to express myself without fear of transgressing from fixed tactical instructions. I wonder what the great Pep Guardiola would have made of Derek Spence the footballer?

Things were going really well at Bury and I seemed to be something of a favourite with Allan Brown. He would say to the rest of the team, "If Derek gets the ball anywhere over the halfway line, he can do whatever he likes!" The downside was that if I received the ball inside my own half, I was supposed to lay it off. That was his way of freeing up the creative side of my football.

I loved Allan Brown as a manager and person. He died a few years ago and I was proud to speak at his funeral. He was quietly spoken and very rarely lost his temper. All the players liked him and he in turn was very loyal to them. And if it suited his purpose, he turned a blind eye to any shenanigans off the pitch.

He wasn't a great tactician but gave me so much confidence. As a young player I had the engine to run all day; chasing lost causes and scoring quite a few goals when clumsy or lazy defenders thought that I was too far away from them to be any threat. They would stroke the ball back to the keeper without putting much oomph into the pass and suddenly I would be tearing up the pitch from some insane position and the race was on. I usually lost, but once in a while I would win the contest and it would result in a goal.

I recall Bury drawing my old club Oldham Athletic in the League Cup. In the game at Boundary Park, Daddy was there to watch me in action having sailed over from Northern Ireland for the occasion. Bury won 3-2 and I scored, against Harry Dowd if my memory serves me correctly, but Daddy's night was even more memorable. One Latics fan, unaware that he was in the company of Billy Spence, hard nut Protestant from Ulster, opined that the ex-Oldham striker Derek Spence was a fucking wanker. After bellowing "that's my fucking son", and disinclined to discuss the matter any further, my Daddy's more eloquent response was to land a juddering right-hand punch which curtailed any further abuse directed my way from that section of the ground.

Somehow, the new players like me managed to gel with the old players and we won promotion to the old third division in my first full season at Bury, despite losing Allan Brown in November 1973 when he took the job of Nottingham Forest manager.

The camaraderie at Bury was amazing, perhaps as a result of our own particular slant on team building. If it was your birthday you had better watch out: you knew the lads were going to do something rotten to you. A low drone would emanate from the changing rooms and morph into a war chant such as those seen in the old Western films. "Hey na na na. Hey na na na. Hey na na na". They didn't actually have tomahawks, but what they did have was plenty of boot polish and they would strip you naked and blacken your bollocks with the polish.

John Forest was a farmer (could you imagine such a thing these days?) and every Thursday he would bring us some eggs. So, if any of the lads had a posh car, you could be sure that as he drove out of the ground on a Thursday, he would suddenly be ambushed by a load of lunatics throwing eggs at his car. Or, if your birthday coincided with egg day, they would rub eggs into your hair and clothes. It was horrendous.

Jimmy Nicholson even climbed up the stanchion of one of the floodlights to escape this treatment on his birthday, but the lads knew he would have to come down in the end, and when he did, they made him pay for delaying their little ritual. Jimmy was incredibly strong and fought like a demon, but he could do little against an entire team.

One time, on my birthday, I thought I would foil them. I dressed in a tracksuit as usual and then I got a length of chain and wrapped it all around myself, locked it with a padlock and then put another, bigger, tracksuit over the lot of it. I don't know what I was trying to achieve really, but once they found the key, which I had hidden in my car, my fate was sealed. It took weeks to get all the boot polish off my bollocks!

The lad who found the padlock key in my car was Steve Hoolikin. He came from a big council estate in Middleton, Manchester but despite his role in the blackening of the Spence bollocks, he went on to become one of my best mates in football, although in recent years his move down to Brighton means that we don't see as much of each other as I'd like.

The team spirit at Bury really was first class. Whenever we went away we would end up having a right laugh. In the early seventies streaking was all the rage and one of the lads, David Holt, did it at Swansea. David went on to be best man at my wedding to Frances, although that day, to the best of my knowledge at least, he remained fully clothed.

When Allan Brown left Bury in November 1973 and Bobby Smith replaced him, I found it impossible to develop the same rapport with the new gaffer. Bobby guided us to promotion and I went on to play under him for almost three years in total, but I was never as happy working with him as I'd been with Brownie.

It was difficult to put my finger on just why I never got on with Bobby Smith. I thought he was okay at first. He always picked me when fit, helped me win my first international call up and was a decent enough manager. But he was a very strict disciplinarian and over time appeared to make it his aim to rid the club of all the players he'd inherited, probably so as to exclude any possibility of them making a bid for his job. After seeing all my mates move on, I too began to feel exposed but back in 1974 I was still loving life at Bury.

The promotion run-in at the denouement of the 1973/74 season should have been a tense, nervy affair, but I loved it. I felt no nerves whatsoever and was supremely confident we'd do it. I had great faith in my team-mates and was never fearful about anything football related back then. It all just felt exciting and when promotion was clinched versus Newport County it was a wonderful feeling. To have worked so hard and achieved tangible success was a great thrill, and we celebrated like it was 1999!

The inevitable post-match celebrations were held in a pub at Holcombe Brook. We always drank with fans after a game and this was to be no different. It was bedlam, with soda siphons going off and pints being poured over one another. The perfect end to what was undoubtedly the happiest time of my career.

Despite my reservations about Bobby Smith, I signed an improved contract in July 1974 and I was raring to go ahead of the 74/75 season in Division Three.

As per usual, I was suspended for the beginning of the campaign and by the time I returned to action in a 3-1 defeat at Wrexham we had won one and lost one in the league but had knocked out my old club Oldham Athletic in the League Cup.

That kind of inconsistency dogged us all season in the league and we finished a respectable but unglamorous 14th.

In the FA Cup we went to the trouble of defeating Millwall after two replays (remember those?) only to then lose to Mansfield Town.

I enjoyed a good season though, scoring twenty goals and was always an automatic choice - if fit and not suspended.

Unbeknown to me, Manchester United's scouts had been having a look at me during the 1974/75 campaign. Tommy Docherty was manager at the time and United were playing in the second division, having been relegated at the end of the previous season. United offered £40,000 for me with a further £20,000 by way of bonus if I got an international cap with Northern Ireland - something that was pretty much guaranteed with the exposure that playing at Man United would create.

However, Bury priced themselves and me out of the market by telling Docherty that he could have me at the princely sum of £100,000. This extravagant valuation brought a typically forthright response from Docherty, "£100,000: I could buy the whole fucking team for that money!" So, as you can imagine, I never went to Old Trafford. Indeed, I was destined never to play a single game in the top-flight, a status United reclaimed after winning the second division title that season.

Blissfully ignorant of such machinations, off the pitch I was trying my hand at being a businessman. I went into partnership with a local insurance salesman by the name of Bernard Whetston, and between us we set up a little travel agency, which we called Whitefield Travel – Whitefield being an area on the outskirts of Bury where we had our office. Lots of footballers were trying to get into business at that time: Colin Bell and a lad called Colin Waldron, who played for Burnley, had a little restaurant just across the road from our office.

I had this idea that as well as being a footballer, I could also be a part-time businessman. I found that I could sell holidays all day long. Talking was never likely to be a problem for me, but when it came to taking bookings and managing the computer side of the business, I was never going to make a go of it. I put a bit of money into the travel agency, but the only thing I ever took out of it was one free holiday per year. Some businessman!

Bernard was a somewhat eccentric person to have as a business partner. For a starter, the office was always staffed by young lads. I had been expecting there to be a team of glamorous girls, all in short skirts and tight blouses but I began to realise that Bernard's tastes were not the same as my own. The penny finally dropped when I invited him to come to the PFA Footballer of the Year award as my guest. I think Bernard took this as a sign that he and I were going to forge a relationship outside the world of the office. What can I say? It must have been all that blond hair of mine.

I retained my interest in Whitefield Travel for about eight or nine years, after which time I decided to cash in my share of the business. The fact is, that I had had very little to do with either Bernard or the business, apart from taking the occasional holiday at cost price. By that time my share of the business was probably worth about 20 thousand pounds or so, but it wasn't cash that I wanted. Bernard had a beautiful Mercedes 450 SL sports car that only had 20,000 miles on the clock. I took the car as payment for my share in the business.

What a disaster. The bloody thing was terrible on fuel economy. I took it over to Belfast on a short visit and the petrol costs alone nearly bankrupted me, so when I got back I put it up for sale and a bloke offered me £20,000 over the phone. I couldn't accept quickly enough.

By this time, I was in a serious relationship with a local girl called Frances and I was also on the brink of an international call up. Even more exciting times awaited.

Chapter 5 [1975 - 1976]
International debut - Fame at last!

1975 was a pivotal year in my life. I got married to Frances, took out my first mortgage, was playing in the third division with Bury after our promotion during season 1973/1974 and, to top it all, on the footballing front at least, I made my international debut for Northern Ireland.

The wedding to Frances took place in Bury's lovely big Church of England edifice with club director, Canon Reg Smith, presiding over the service. Dave Holt was my best man and all of my team-mates attended, as of course did my family. It was a fantastic day, followed by a honeymoon in Cornwall, only made possible because I was serving a customary suspension after totting up yet more bookings.

On the strength of my performances that season with Bury, I received my first call up for the Northern Ireland squad in April 1975. Perhaps the player-manager, Dave Clements, had heard rumours of Manchester United's purported interest in me. Possibly, he had even heard of my alleged £100,000 valuation! Which is more than I fucking did!

Whatever the reason, I was invited to take part in a practice game with the national squad at Bellfield, which was Everton's training ground.

Billy Bingham was manager of Everton and Clements was also an Everton player, so it was probably through them that this practice match was set up. It was played behind closed doors and one of its purposes was to let Dave Clements have a look at me. I was still very raw but naturally I was mad keen to impress. And of course, it was a great opportunity to meet and play with established stars like Pat Jennings and Sammy McIlroy.

I remember being in the changing rooms before the match, with the team still to be announced. The manager came in and revealed that he had picked me to spearhead our forward line and handed me the much coveted and iconic number nine shirt.

As we were getting changed, word went around that we were to receive a visit from footballing royalty: Bill Shankly. The great man lived - somewhat ironically - close to Everton's training ground.

Sure enough Shanks came into the dressing room and was having a word of encouragement with all the lads, many of whom he knew as established stars of the first division. He started off with the goalie and then the defenders and when he came to me, I shook his hand. In his unmistakeable lowland Scots drawl he said to me, "A good firm handshake you've got there sonny: not like some of these nancy boys!" I was bursting with pride that he had taken the time to add those extra words and I felt about seven feet tall. Looking back on it now, I realise that he was just trying to calm the nerves of the raw rookie, but I will never forget that moment. I guess too that Shanks, in common with many, was secretly willing the kid from the lower divisions to do well and force his way into an international team mainly composed of first division footballers.

Buoyed by this encouragement, I took to the field where I was up against a rising star in Everton's first team: defender Mark Higgins. I gave poor old Mark a torrid time. I was all over him like a cheap suit. I scored two goals and generally caused mayhem in Everton's 18-yard box. We beat Everton by five goals. Perhaps Mark had been unable to work up too much enthusiasm for his task, marking a third division player, but complacency is harshly punished in football and so it was on that day.

On the strength of that performance I was picked for our upcoming European Championship qualifier against Yugoslavia (as they were then known); Northern Ireland's first home game for almost five years; a hiatus due solely to the impact of the 'Troubles'.

The game was to be played at five o'clock on a Sunday afternoon, an inconvenient time that was picked in an attempt to lessen any possible disruptions. And, as a bitter blow to the home fans, there was to be no drinking allowed inside the ground!

Belfast seldom had a good image during `The Troubles' but the 1970's marked an all-time low in its appeal to visitors from Britain and overseas. Bombings, shootings, religious sectarianism and political strife ensured that Belfast was low on any outsider's must-see bucket list.

Another group conspicuous by their absence on Northern Irish soil, were international footballers. Not since the Soviet Union in October 1971 had a national side dared to set foot in the Province. Everyone understood why, but it was a depressing reminder of our country's isolation and threatened the entire existence of the national side.

Then, astonishingly, Yugoslavia agreed to visit. The excitement was palpable and on the afternoon of the match thousands of people converged on Windsor Park. Before my move to England, I'd been a regular at Windsor Park, but I'd never seen such crowds in Belfast before, not outside the marching season at least.

As the team bus approached Windsor Park, I looked around and saw the building sites I had worked on as a joiner just five years earlier. Now I was coming back home as a fully-fledged international. I was 22 years old and had just got married and bought my first house. I'd helped my club to win promotion and the press were linking me with clubs that would catapult me into the highest echelons of the domestic game. Things had certainly changed dramatically for me.

Naturally, I was pretty nervous, even with the passionate backing of 40,000 Northern Irish to offer me succour. Somewhere in the crowd, Daddy and the rest of my family were roaring their encouragement. Indeed, I think that was the only game my sister Isabella ever attended. She hated football then and still does, although I'm sure I could hear her screams of encouragement even above the din of the rest of the crowd.

At ten to five when the teams emerged from the tunnel, a cold, grey April evening was transformed into a carnival. The match itself was always going to struggle to live up to such a build-up and, for a while, it proved a dull and cagey affair.

The Yugoslavs looked like a race of giants. I remember looking at one of them, a well-known player at the time called Josip Katalinski, and wondering if there was any end to this fella. He just seemed to go up and up. Not only was he tall, but he was built like a brick shithouse. During the game itself, I heard one old schoolmate shout out "kick the fuck out of him Snowball". As if.

Subsequently, when I went back to Yugoslavia a few years later, I mentioned Katalinski's name a couple of times and he was clearly well thought of as I can't remember having to buy another drink once I told people I had played against the big fella. I subsequently learned that Katalinski, a Bosnian, had become a national hero 12 months before my encounter with him after scoring the goal that clinched qualification for the 1974 World Cup during which Yugoslavia clashed with Scotland. He was also one of those rare breeds who, during the communist era, played abroad, finishing his career in France with Nice.

In the end we beat Yugoslavia 1-0 with Bryan Hamilton notching our goal. I didn't score, but I had a goal disallowed for being (fractionally) offside. I was happy with my performance and delighted to have been part of a historic occasion. And this was not just any old team of muppets flown in to make up the numbers. Yugoslavia was one of the most talented footballing nations in Europe at that time.

The press reacted to my display positively. One match report opined that Northern Ireland's best performer was the previously unknown Derek Spence of Bury who, with his blond feather-cut, looked about 16 but gave the revered Slav defence a torrid time. The report concluded by stating that poised, sophisticated players who could hold their own against the best strikers in the world, couldn't handle a kid from north Belfast.

My family were clearly proud of me but, as ever, didn't go overboard in their praise, believing I needed to keep my feet firmly on the ground. Daddy in particular never said much, but from that day on his life changed too with people frequently wanting to talk to him about his footballing son. I know though that he loved talking about my exploits and even when strangers knocked on his door asking him to get my autograph for them he never turned anyone away or objected to the intrusion.

My sisters were also delighted at my breakthrough, as of course was Frances, who regularly attended my matches until our first child was born. The fact that my wife and family had shared this great occasion with me made it all the more precious.

Bury chairman, Billy Allen, had flown over to Belfast to watch the game. I am sure he too had been impressed with my performance and was no doubt rubbing his hands at the prospect of a big offer for my services.

The incongruous nature of my club status compared to my team-mates is underlined when you consider the make-up of the the Northern Ireland team versus Yugoslavia on that historic evening of 16 April 1975 and the clubs they then played for:

Pat Jennings (Tottenham Hotspur), Pat Rice (Arsenal), Sammy Nelson (Arsenal), Chris Nicholl (Aston Villa), Allan Hunter (Ipswich Town), Dave Clements (Everton), Bryan Hamilton (Ipswich Town), Martin O'Neill (Nottingham Forest), Derek Spence (Bury), Sammy McIlroy (Manchester United), Tommy Jackson (Nottingham Forest).

If I thought that my international debut was to be the ultimate thrill, the Home Internationals, as was then customary, began at the end of the domestic club season and so began one of the most memorable seven days of my career.

Our campaign began with a game at Windsor Park versus England. The line-ups that day were as follows:

Northern Ireland: Pat Jennings, Pat Rice, Liam O'Kane, Chris Nicholl, Allan Hunter, Dave Clements, Bryan Hamilton, Martin O'Neill, Derek Spence, Sammy McIlroy, Tommy Jackson. Sub: Tommy Finney.

England: Ray Clemence, Steve Whitworth, Emlyn Hughes, Colin Bell, Dave Watson, Colin Todd, Alan Ball, Colin

Viljoen, Malcolm MacDonald, Kevin Keegan, Dennis Tueart. Sub: Micky Channon.

The game ended in a goalless draw but the match was anything but dull. And for me, the game changed my life in many ways. I was given the man of the match award and for the first time in my career became known to the football public at large.

The much-respected journalist Brian Glanville, for the Sunday Times, eulogised at length about my performance: "The remarkable Derek Spence, ran wild and free, setting all kinds of problems for a far from composed England defence. Spence set up a great chance for Sammy McIlroy which Ray Clemence saved. The young centre forward - blonde as a Swede - went close himself with a shot which went just wide and seemed unaffected by the fact that he had come straight out of the third division. The Irish played with the dash, heart and commitment one traditionally associates with them making the most of the relatively little they have got, while in the surprising Spence, who left the field waving his delight, they had perhaps the game's most appealing player. He may not be a player of great finesse but he is quick, brave and persistent both on the ground and in the air. Lanky and leggy, Spence must have added at least £50,000 more to his transfer fee".

Post-match, I was quoted as saying that I didn't think I had played as well in that game as against Yugoslavia but hadn't let anyone down. What an amazingly humble boy I was!

The crowd was 35,000 and it was interesting to learn from a friend, Paul Cambridge, who has assisted me in writing this book, just how much of an impact that game had in relation to my becoming a more prominent figure in British football. Paul remembers this game almost better than I do and said that many football fans of his age group were captivated by the exploits of a previously unknown lower division footballer who outshone even the great Kevin Keegan that day.

Mind you, Keegan was to dominate the headlines the following week when he petulantly stormed out of the England HQ having been left out of the team to play Wales. Don Revie eventually cajoled him back in time for KK to star at Wembley as England crushed Scotland 5-1 to clinch the Home Internationals title.

Four days after the England tie, Northern Ireland travelled to Glasgow to face Scotland and were defeated 3-0. I again played the full 90 minutes, but it was definitely one of those "falling down to earth with a bump" experiences.

Our final game of the series was back in Belfast against Wales, which we won 1-0 with a goal from Tom Finney. So, three starts and no goals for yours truly but plenty of headlines for "Snowball, the kid with long blonde locks", and as season 1975/76 lurked on the horizon there were plenty of newspaper stories linking me with a move to a new club.

Despite my semi-celebrity status, life remained much the same as before. My old friends took the piss a bit more, presumably to ensure I kept my feet on the ground, I seemed to become even more interesting to certain females, and I was asked to do more charity work in Bury. Mind you, I'd always enjoyed doing this and anyway believed it to be part of my job as a Bury footballer so, being the great bloke I was, I was happy to immerse myself in such work after training.

As my career developed, visits to the family back home in Northern Ireland became more sporadic. My parents and siblings were always proud of my achievements and despite my frequent absences from their lives we remained close and on good terms throughout.

Chapter 6 [October 1976]
Bestie and me - Biggest game of my career

Throughout my career, and in-spite of my volcanic temper, I was sent off just once. This came for Bury versus Gillingham in October 1973. A record I am reasonably proud of to be honest, although in todays' game I'd have taken an early bath far more frequently I think.

But I collected bookings like Green Shield stamps and at the start of the 1976/77 season, as was often the case, I was suspended for having amassed too many disciplinary points. But apart from that minor inconvenience, I was looking forward to bigger and better things.

My plans were temporarily undone when I suffered a badly torn thigh muscle in a reserve team game. This was a really nasty injury and I had a bloody great lump on the top of my thigh to contend with. The physio at Bury was not really equipped to deal with such a potentially career-threatening injury, so I had to go to Manchester City for some help. Their physiotherapist, Freddie Griffiths, was great, and as soon as he had a look at my leg he arranged an operation - the very next day at Manchester Royal Infirmary. The urgency with which all this was sorted out tells you just how serious it might have been had I not had the right treatment immediately.

During my recuperation I was down at City's ground every day doing my rehab under the supervision of Freddie. I spent long hours in their hot Jacuzzi-type baths, which must have done the trick, because I was back playing again in two weeks.

There was definitely some pressure from Bury to get me back into the first team and playing again. I was pushed back into action before I was really ready, and six games later I was still struggling to achieve full match fitness.

Despite of this, I got picked again for the Northern Ireland squad to face the Dutch in Holland on 13 October 1976 for a World Cup qualifier. This was at a time when the Dutch were one of the top teams in world football, having a team fairly bristling with superstars: Cruyff, Neeskens and the rest. Not only that, but George Best - now wowing the fans of Fulham at Craven Cottage - had also been picked to join the team after some time out of the international picture following his premature retirement whilst at Manchester United. So, no pressure for Bury FC's humble centre forward then.

Since the 1975 Home Internationals, I had started four games and made one substitute appearance.

I had played the full 90 minutes on 3 September 1975 versus Sweden in Belfast, when we narrowly lost a World Cup qualifier 2-1, but I wasn't selected for the next two games – both of which we lost - before earning a recall for another World Cup qualifier against Israel on 3 March 1976.

This was to be my sixth cap and I was still seeking my first international goal. Mind you, since my debut against Yugoslavia the previous year, Northern Ireland had scored just twice in six games, a run which included three defeats and a draw, so my rivals for a striking role were not proving any more effective in front of goal than I was. Nevertheless, as a striker you are judged on the goals you score and I was desperate to break my duck.

The Israel game ended in a 1-1 draw with Tom Finney scoring for us. I played the full 90 minutes and again drew a blank in front of goal, but one surprising spin-off from that trip was a chance encounter with ex model Mandy Rice-Davies in a Tel Aviv bar.

I was with Jimmy Nicholl - one of my best mates in football - and we both readily recognised the beautiful ex show girl. Mandy, of course, had been a prominent figure in the 1960's Profumo scandal when, as an associate of Christine Keeler, she became embroiled in a notorious sequence of events which led to John Profumo, a Government Minister, resigning his post and Keeler and Rice Davies becoming household names.

Rice Davies later traded on her notoriety, even comparing herself to Nelson's mistress, Lady Hamilton, but by that night in Tel Aviv she had married an Israeli businessman, Rafi Shauli, converted to Judaism and seemed far removed from the infamous figure she had once been

I was back on the bench for the opening match in the 1976 Home International series when on 8 May 1976 we made the worst possible start, losing 3-0 to Scotland at Hampden Park. I came on for Sammy Morgan but had little chance to impress.

I received a huge boost just three days later when I started against England at Wembley. I did well enough to see out the full 90 minutes, but we suffered another heavy defeat; Mike Channon with a brace and Stuart Pearson and Gerry Francis also scoring in a comprehensive 4-0 victory for the host team. I was up against Colin Todd who had a magnificent game. What a player Todd was, definitely one of the best defenders I played against. Very fast, cool as a cucumber and hard as nails.

As I was coming off the pitch at the end, I heard someone call out "Alright Snowball? You look fucked son". It was my old childhood mate and neighbour, Colin Noble, now based in England as a policeman and undertaking match duties that day.

The final game of the series took place on 14 May 1976 against Wales at the Vetch Field. The match was meaningless for us results wise because our two previous defeats had left us out of the running for the title, but I was delighted to again earn a starting role, only to be replaced by Morgan in a frustrating game which the Welsh won via a Leighton James strike.

This poor run, and the perception that the squad was ill-disciplined and lacked focus, led to Dave Clements being replaced by Danny Blanchflower and Dave moving to the United States where he ended his playing career in 1978.

Despite Danny being a massive hero of mine and someone I was excited to work with, I was desperately sorry to see Dave go. He had given me my debut, believed in me when others wrote me off as a lower division also-ran, and I liked him as a lad too. He was still a first division player with Everton when handed the dual role as player manager of Northern Ireland so, as a peer member of the group, it was always going to be difficult for him to instil discipline in a squad that was always ready to party.

The Holland encounter was to be our first international of the 1976/77 season and after a dreadful run of results we were expected to be on the wrong end of another trouncing.

Danny arranged a warm-up against Coventry City. The players assembled in a Coventry hotel the night before the game. Now, as it happens, I had met George Best previously, but not in the capacity of a colleague. I had been in Manchester to watch a game and had caught a glimpse of him outside his famous and eponymous boutique on Bridge

Street and I had asked him for his autograph. There was a brief conversation and a bit of banter, but I was just a kid and he was a superstar.

Jimmy Nicholl introduced me to Bestie in a hotel bar in Coventry and, me being me, I mentioned the fact that it was not, in fact, our first meeting. Gentleman that he was, he claimed to remember our encounter, but I am sure that, in reality, I had been to him just another star struck kid with an autograph book.

I offered to buy him a drink, but he refused saying that the drinks were on him. Whereupon, he pulled out a wad of notes that would have choked a donkey and went to the bar and bought a huge round. We got to talking tactics for our game the next day. It looked like I was going to start the game on the bench. But I could hardly complain about being ousted from the team by George Best.

And it wasn't just on the pitch where Bestie was a legend. We had been having a drink in the residents' bar in our hotel. The barmaid was absolutely stunning and somehow or other, although I never saw him speak to her, at the end of the evening, as we were saying our goodnights, this girl suddenly appeared out of thin air alongside the great man and off they went into the night.

As I feared, I started the game as a substitute. As Bestie ran past me onto the pitch he called out, "count how many nutmegs I get!" And every time he humiliated an opponent with that particular move, he would look my way and shout, "Are you counting?" This was Danny Blanchflower's first, albeit unofficial, game in charge of the national squad and we won 8-0.

Danny was greatly inspired by the Dutch style of football and his mantra was, "attack, attack, attack!" Naturally this philosophy was music to my ears but our new manager and my erstwhile hero was something of a footballing snob if truth be told and unless you were playing regular first team football in the first division, you were unlikely to get much of a look in. Even players who couldn't get into their own first teams were preferred to second and third division players, as for some reason he reckoned that being with a first division football club, even at reserve team level, conveyed some kind of kudos.

I thought his attitude was bollocks. A lot of lads who find themselves in that situation end up getting released by their clubs. To my mind, regular first-team football is a far better indicator of class, even in the lower divisions.

In the end, I never got on the pitch during the Coventry game, but I did count the nutmegs and George must have got about 20 of them against his bamboozled markers.

After the game we both went out on to the pitch for a bit of a crossbar challenge. George hit the crossbar five or six times consecutively, without even seeming to think about how he was going to strike the ball. There is no fluke about that level of skill.

A short while later, we flew out to Rotterdam to face the mighty Dutch. Danny Blanchflower, who must have fancied himself as some sort of Irish Yves Saint Laurent, had even designed a new kit for the occasion. With regards to his sartorial talents you could probably say that as a designer he made a good football manager.

With our new attacking attitude and our new strip, there was plenty of excitement, and speculation was rife as to whether I was going to start the game or not.

Some things, though, never change. Before the game, the phone rang in our room and my room-mate Jimmy Nicholl answered.

It was Blackpool manager Allan Brown and he wanted to speak to me, but what he got was Jimmy Nicholl pretending to be me. Naturally, Jimmy thought it was somebody else trying to wind us up. Jimmy was saying, "Oh yes, Allan, I'd love to come to Blackpool!" And all the while Allan thought he was actually talking to me. Eventually it dawned on Jimmy that the call was real. At about the same time as it dawned on Allan that he had not been talking to me! Eventually I managed to get a word in and found that Blackpool wanted to sign me and I agreed to meet Brownie on my return to England.

I was doubly excited in Rotterdam, chuffed to bits about the prospect of playing against the Dutch, and thrilled too about a possible move to Blackpool. Things were on the up and up for this boy from a Belfast council estate.

I was on the bench. I swallowed my disappointment by being as supportive as possible in the dug-out. The lads gave it everything and incredibly we were soon winning 1–0, thanks to a goal by Chris McGrath, a regular in Manchester United's reserve side. There was no denying that we were living up to our pre-match promise to deliver attacking football, but in the second half the Dutch came back with a great strike from Ruud Krol who buried the ball in the back of the net from fully 35thirty-five yards out. Big Pat Jennings never had a chance with that one.

Then our mercurial talisman, George Best, got the ball and went off on a storming run, which ended up, after he had nutmegged Johan Neeskens no less, with him losing the ball. The great Johan Cruyff was suddenly bearing down on our goal. He took a shot and his initial attempt was palmed away by Jennings, but the Dutchman was not one of the world's top players for nothing, and as he pounced on the rebound we were 2-1 down and facing defeat.

I got the shout to say I was going on for my 10th cap and I have never warmed up so fast in my life. I couldn't wait to get on that pitch and within ten minutes of coming on, the Dutch keeper parried a cross from David McCreery and spilled the ball at my feet on the edge of the box. In those situations, the last thing a striker needs to hear is a lone voice crying out, "Leave it!" The last thing I was going to do was to fucking well leave it. I wellied it straight into the back of the net!

That goal was the finest moment of my sporting career. Not only had I scored my first goal for my country against the legendary Dutch team, but to add to the occasion, my idol, George Best, threw his arms around me and congratulated me on my goal. Talk about living the dream.

After that, Bestie picked up the ball again, beat about four Dutch players and then succeeded in being dispossessed as he had a few minutes earlier. As he jogged past me a second or so later, I bellowed at him, "For fuck's sake pass!" The occasion must have got to me, because I couldn't really believe that I was giving a bollocking to the greatest footballer ever to play for Northern Ireland. After the game ended, in the euphoria of having got a draw in Rotterdam, I collected my thoughts and apologised to the great man. To my surprise, he replied thus, "Oh, you were right, I should have passed!" He truly was a great bloke.

When not chastising legends, I was charging round the dressing room with a little instamatic camera taking pictures of anybody who would stand still long enough. I was mad about taking pictures at that time and rarely went anywhere without my wee camera.

I was ecstatic. I had proved that lower division footballers - this one for sure - could make it at international level against the great teams and players. Many of my team-mates that night were not even regulars at first-team level for their clubs but the fact that they were employed by big name clubs was all too often the deciding factor in team selection. David McCreery - who had a blinder that night man-marking Johan Cruyff - was a rare starter for Manchester United, as was the case for Tommy Jackson.

But the Bury player from Division Three had come up with the goods on this occasion and I hoped fervently that this was just the start for me. My first international goal on my tenth appearance and hopefully many more to come in the future.

For the record, the respective teams that night in Rotterdam were as follows:

Holland: Eddy Treijtel, Wim Rijsbergen, Ruud Krol, Adri Van Kraay, Arie Haan, Wim Jansen, Johan Neeskens, Johan Cruyff, Ruud Geels, Willy Van Der Kerkhof, Rob Rensenbrink. Subs: Rene Van Der Kerkhof and Willy Van Der Kuylen.

Northern Ireland: Pat Jennings, Jimmy Nicholl, Pat Rice, Tommy Jackson, Allan Hunter, Bryan Hamilton, Sammy McIlroy, George Best, Chris McGrath, David McCreery, Trevor Anderson. Sub: Derek Spence.

Holland duly qualified from our group for the 1978 World Cup, reaching the final against the host nation, Argentina, losing a bad tempered final 3-1. The great Cruyff retired from international football before those finals but several of his team-mates that night went on to star in the competition, including Krol, Haan, Neeskens and the Van Der Kerkhof twins, while Rensenbrink scored Holland's goal in the final versus Argentina.

This great side lost two consecutive World Cup finals but were undoubtedly one of the greatest teams of that era and that match and my goal were undoubtedly the high spots of my career.

After the game, we went back to the team hotel and within about an hour everybody was pissed. Let's face it, a team of Irishmen was unlikely to let a result like that go uncelebrated. The festivities remain largely a blur in my memory, apart from one incident. I was in bed at about four in the morning and one of the lads burst into the room and soaked me with a fire hose.

A good drink and a lack of sleep combined to ensure that I looked awful when it came to the next phase of my career: signing for Blackpool in London.

Despite being linked to numerous clubs, I had remained a Bury player for the entirety of the 1975/76 season. I was disappointed, especially when a move to Brian Clough's soon to be all conquering Nottingham Forest failed to materialise - one of many 'what if', sliding doors moments in my career - but I vowed to get my head down and produce my best for Bury in the hope that a move to a bigger club would happen at some point. After all, I was still reasonably happy at Bury, the fans loved me, my wife was a local girl, and we were planning to start a family.

I signed what turned out to be my last Bury contract in July 1975, again just for one season on wages of £80 per week, plus some reasonably handsome bonuses in recognition of my new-found international status.

I had a decent enough season personally, scoring ten league and cup goals in 35 appearances but with Bury finishing way off the Division Three promotion pace in 13th. I was growing stale and longed for a move to a bigger club.

That season, we won just 14 games and drew 18. My nine league goals were approximately a fifth of the entire team output as we hit the back of the net just 51 times. Many of my old team-mates had now moved on, I was more disenchanted with Bobby Smith than ever, and the only thing keeping me going were the fantastic Bury fans.

It was not until October of the following season, in the immediate aftermath of the Holland game, that I finally got my wish for a move, although sadly it still wasn't the First Division which beckoned, but Blackpool in the second tier. Nevertheless, it was still a step up as my new club were considered to be genuine promotion candidates, so I hoped that one day soon I'd finally get my chance to play at the highest level domestically.

All in all, I had loved my time at Bury. I genuinely adored the fans, the town itself, and I think I did a good job for the club as my 44 goals in 140 appearances demonstrate.

I'd helped the club win promotion from the fourth division, played for my country, got married, and found my feet in a new country.

But it was time for a new challenge.

Chapter 7 [1976-1977]
Seasiders Part 1 - Blackpool FC

I had loved my time at Bury but when the chance came to join Blackpool it was a move I couldn't turn down.

I was genuinely delighted to join Blackpool. I still hadn't made it to the top-flight but the 'Seasiders' were one of the top teams in the second division at the time, and although they had just missed out on promotion during season 1975/76 they were flying high and had some of the biggest names ever to play for the club. Players like Bob Hatton, Alan Ainscough, Micky Walsh, Paul Hart, George Wood, and the late, great Alan Suddick, who many people reckon was one of the greatest players never to win an England cap.

Alan was famous for his swerving free kicks, long before David Beckham and Cristiano Ronaldo. I believe he also held the world record for keepie-uppies, doing any number of laps of Bloomfield Road whilst keeping a ball in mid-air. Alan was a famously relaxed character and I can never remember him making a tackle, but why should he get involved in that side of the game when he had all that talent?

Alan was a really genuine fella and lived in a little terraced house close to Blackpool's ground. Even when he was being idolised by the fans he never let his ego get too big and would still undertake little painting and decorating jobs for people.

After his football career ended, he worked as a painter and decorator right up until the time he contracted the cancer which sadly took his life. The last time I saw Blackpool's most famous free kick specialist was at Revoe Park in the south end of Blackpool. He was already quite ill by this time, but even though it must have been apparent to him how things were going to turn out, he remained positive, talking about his fervent wish to get out on the golf course once again.

Unfortunately, he never got his wish. Hundreds of Blackpudlians turned out for his funeral: a fitting tribute to the man justly known by the regal title - King of Bloomfield Road.

My old boss Allan Brown had recently been appointed to the manager's job at Blackpool, having left Southport who he had managed briefly following his dismissal by Nottingham Forest in 1975 when he was replaced by Brian Clough.

I met my former Bury gaffer in a hotel in London, where I duly signed a contract that would start from that October to the end of the 1977/78 season. The Blackpool move increased my wages to £100 a week, so things were looking pretty rosy. The only fly in the ointment was the fact that I would be taking over from the hugely popular Alan Suddick.

Blackpool paid £50,000 for me, and Oldham got a percentage of that, as they had been canny enough to put a sell-on clause in my contract with them. On top of my basic was a bonus of a further £100 per point for any wins we might get whilst we were in the top four of the division, which we were for pretty much all the season, meaning my move to Blackpool effectively trebled the money I had been on at Bury.

A little while later I had to go back to Bury to sort out some monies they owed me. They had cocked up all my tax codes, so that first week at Blackpool I was taxed as if I was one of the Beatles. I always felt this accident was, in fact, anything but an accident.

Not only that, but they owed me some money for getting international caps, as every time I played for my country, I was representing Bury as well. I reckoned they owed me about £900, but I came away from the meeting with just a fraction of that. Bury had subbed me £500 when I first got there and was a bit short of readies. I was assured at the time that it would be forgotten about, but they had long memories when it came to monies they reckoned I owed and they deducted it in the blink of an eye.

My job now though was to concentrate on Blackpool. They played a 4-3-3 formation with three strikers up front. Bob Hatton was one of them and alongside him was Micky Walsh, who was their star striker at the time. Mickey was a great favourite with the fans and later went on to enjoy spells with Everton and FC Porto. I was the third man in the trio and I was going to be playing out on the left to bring a bit of width to the attack.

At Bury I had been a big fish in a small pond, but at Blackpool the tables were turned which suited me as I had never craved stardom. I bought a house in Preesall, which is in the rural Over-Wyre district: the land on the opposite side of the River Wyre from Blackpool. This is a farming area, far removed from the temptations of Britain's best-known seaside resort, so whilst my colleagues were regulars in all the town's nightclubs I opted for the quiet life in my rural hideaway. Blackpool had a very successful season that year and just missed out on promotion to the first division.

I made my debut against Brian Clough's Nottingham Forest team, who went up as champions that year. We beat them 1 - 0 at home and I can clearly remember that Martin O'Neil played in that game. I knew Martin from the Holland game, in which he had also played, and he remains a friend to this day.

Although I was predominantly a right-footed player, Allan Brown had me playing on the left of the park all season. It came as no surprise then, when at the end of the season the boss announced he was going to adopt the more traditional 4-4-2 formation, it was me who found himself surplus to requirements! But at least Allan Brown told me honestly in a face-to-face meeting which I appreciated.

I was gutted and couldn't face joining another English club so soon after my previous move, so I rang up a few footballing journalists I knew and let them know that I wanted a move abroad. This was the summer of 1977 and well before the time Irish and British players like Liam Brady, Trevor Francis, Graeme Souness, Ian Rush, Mark Hughes made playing abroad fashionable, albeit temporarily, for UK based footballers.

Why I wanted to move overseas so badly I'm not sure. I simply recall really fancying going abroad and sampling a different way of life. It helped that Frances was up for it and that we didn't have any kids to worry about, although Frances was to imminently discover that she was pregnant with our first child. And the money sounded attractive too.

Journalist Norman Wynn was especially helpful and whilst I waited for news, I joined in with pre-season training at Blackpool so as to ensure that I would be fit if I got a call.

One night I was sitting at home, when the phone rang. A foreign voice declared himself to be a "Mr Jacobs" and naturally I thought it was one of the lads with yet another wind-up. Both Micky Walsh and Steve Harrison, another fellow player at Blackpool and destined later to be Graham

Taylor's number two with England, were great ones for taking the piss and I wouldn't have put it past them to come up with a ruse like this. So it took me quite a while to work out that the call was genuine.

Anyway, the mysterious Mr. Jacobs asked me if I would like to fly out to Belgium - to FC Bruges. Fuck it: why not!

The next day, I was called into the office in Blackpool where they told me that I was expected to drive down to Southend and from there I was to fly to Bruges. It was like something out of a James Bond film and naturally, I imagined that FC Bruges was going to be involved in this somehow or other.

To cut a long story short, the next thing I knew, I was getting ready for action in the changing room at FC Bruges. A little fella came into the dressing room, grabbed a bag of balls and told me to meet him out on the pitch, where another player was already waiting for me. The first fella asked me if I could get the ball in the net from where I was standing, some 30 yards away.

Given that there was nobody in goals I didn't think it was too much of a challenge. After I had banged in a few shots, the first bloke asked me if I could beat the other fella in one-on-one situations, so after I skinned this big donkey a few times and even nutmegged him for good measure, it appeared that I had passed this rudimentary examination of my skills and the little fella was happy.

It eventually transpired that the little bloke was a certain Mr Takani, a former international striker with the Hungarian national team. He obviously knew his football and he was just as clearly pleased with my results in his little test. Once I had showered and changed back into my civvies, things got seriously weird. Mr Takani examined my knees and gave them a good going over; prodding and poking them as if I were a horse. He then repeated this examination with my ankles and pronounced himself well pleased. At that point things moved from the merely weird to the downright surreal.

Mr Takani might well have known his football, but he didn't have much of a grasp of the English language. When he referred to himself he used the word 'you', and it didn't help matters that he used the same pronoun when he referred to me. But somehow an image formed out of the linguistic mists. Somebody, somewhere, wanted me to play for Olympiacos. I had no idea where that was, so he had to tell me that they were a Greek team. But when he offered a big wad of notes, plus £300 a week, plus all flights and a furnished apartment, I would have signed for Timbuktu Academicals.

The multi-talented Mr Takani turned out to be some sort of forerunner of today's football agent. He had a good day when I signed for Olympiacos, because at the same time they signed a Danish International by the name of Sorensen. Blackpool got £50,000 for me. I got a signing on fee of £20,000, which I put into a Belgian bank account. I later worked out that Olympiacos had probably been willing to go to £100,000 for me: any remaining money represented Mr Takani's fee. Given that he probably repeated this feat with Sorensen, I reckon he earned about £60,000 for his day's work. With today's astronomical fees, it is not hard to work out why so many people are keen to become football agents.

The deal was finalised when, a short time later, Mr Takani met a representative of Blackpool at an airport in London and handed him a suitcase which contained fifty grand in cash. I had just become an Olympiacos player and thus opened one of the most interesting chapters in my footballing career.

My first spell at Blackpool did not prove to be as successful as I'd hoped but I still enjoyed some memorable moments, most notably in a game at promotion rivals Chelsea which finished in a 2-2 draw. The late Ray `Butch' Wilkins played that day for the Londoners, Steve Harrison kicked out at Chelsea's Ian Britton and made headlines in the newspapers as a result, there was a pitch invasion by the notorious members of the `Shed' and I scored a cracking header. Football was rarely televised live in those days but both the BBC and ITV showed extensive highlights of first and second division games and this was one is still replayed today on BT Sport when they feature classic games from earlier decades.

I made many friends during this brief spell at Bloomfield Road, lads like goalkeeper George Wood who later played for Everton and Scotland, another ex-Toffees ace, Alan Ainscough who I still see on occasions, David Hockaday, who shot to national prominence when appointed as Leeds United manager for an ill-fated brief spell, centre half Paul Hart who went on to enjoy a long playing and managerial career, and the late Billy Ronson.

I can't leave this chapter of my career without mentioning one other team-mate that season. Steve Harrison was unquestionably the best joker I ever encountered in football. He was incredibly funny and had us constantly in stiches.

After quitting as a player, Steve joined forces with Graham Taylor and became one of his most foremost coaches and, inevitably, when Taylor got the England job, Harrison became his assistant. Briefly!

One of Steve's party tricks from his tenure at Blackpool involved a glass and his ability to, well, shit into it from a great height. On overnight stays in hotels before away games, Steve would invite team-mates to his room and then perform his unique act. Basically, he selected the highest point in the room - usually the top of a cupboard – line up a glass on the carpet well below him, crouch over the edge of said cupboard, and then shat directly into the goblet. In order to ensure the success of his enterprise and avoid any nasty accidents on the carpet, he would first take a piss in order to assure himself that the glass was correctly lined up. If he missed the first time, he made sure the second was deadly accurate and he never, ever, crapped on the carpet. Which as I'm sure you will agree was very thoughtful of him.

Now most of the civilised world would find this form of behaviour unsavoury to say the least, disgusting even, but footballers found it hilarious, yours truly included, and the prank never lost its appeal for Steve's devoted audiences up and down the land.

Unfortunately, Steve's demonstration of this highly accomplished stunt was not as well received by his new employers at the FA, and after word got around that Harrison had performed it for England's finest in his hotel room, he was summarily sacked.

To my eternal regret, no pictures exist so I will leave it you dear readers to use your imagination if you so wish to explore the depths of your mind and re-live for yourself this incredible experience.

Chapter 8 [1977-1978]
Greece is the word is the word - Olympiacos

Naturally, after I had been scouted by a Hungarian and signed in Belgium to play for a Greek team, our pre-season training was in Germany.

I immediately flew out to Germany from Manchester to meet my new Greek teammates and, continuing the surreal theme, the only team-mate who could speak any English was a Danish player, Nils Sorensen, who they had also signed via the unorthodox offices of Mr Takani.

I was incredibly excited. Frances was due to join me in Greece as soon as humanly possible but for now was presiding over more prosaic affairs at home such as packing.

We left our Blackpool home empty and team-mate Billy Ronson was supposed to be supervising the sale of my Ford Capri (not a white one though before you conjure up an image of Dennis Waterman in the opening credits to 'Minder'). Eventually after failing to sell it for me he instead bought it off me. Great lad Billy, and I was hugely saddened when he died so prematurely in 2015 aged just 58.

I had already done four weeks pre-season training in England, so after another four weeks in Germany I was as fit as a butcher's dog and raring to go. The Greek season starts in late September because of the summer heat. Our training would start at seven in the morning with weights and medicine ball work, followed by a light breakfast at about nine, after which we would be sent to run up and down some nearby hills before lunch. After a siesta we would do ball skills work in the evening, with work on set pieces, drills and little friendly games against some of the local teams. After a month we flew back to Greece, fit and ready to start the season.

I had never visited Greece before - not even on holiday - and the first thing that struck me when I got off the plane in Athens was the heat. I wondered even then if I was ever going to be able to play in those scorching temperatures.

We still managed to get in a handful of friendly games and I scored a few goals. I was keen to let my new colleagues know that I could find the net and was delighted with the start I'd made.

Olympiacos normally played their home games at eight o'clock in the evening, by which time the temperature has dropped. It was actually a joy to play football in those conditions. Even for friendly games Olympiacos attracted crowds of 50,000. The atmosphere inside their stadium was electric and when I made my home debut, I was chaired from one end of the pitch to the other on the shoulders of the adoring fans. Draped in scarves and smothered in kisses I thought they had perhaps mistaken me for the Messiah when really I was just a naughty proddy from Belfast. A far cry from my days at Oldham Athletic certainly.

There were only three major teams in the top tier of Greek football at that time and we played one of them, AEK Athens, in the big Athens derby in one of my early games. It was a friendly and Olympiacos were doing well and so was I, until I slid in on the half-way line to block a ball and my opponent crashed into me with his studs showing. He caught me full on the knee and the pain was awful. I carried on hobbling about for a few minutes, desperate to keep on playing and to show the Greeks the kind of stuff I was made of, but I knew that I was trying to play on with what was actually a serious injury. In the end I had to come off and it looked like I was going to be out for quite a while.

I never properly understood my diagnosis; all I knew was that, with the bizarre Greek treatment regime, taking tablets of every colour of the rainbow and being shuttled about from one incomprehensible specialist to the next, it was going to be a bloody long time before I was match fit. After a while I think I had seen every private doctor in Greece and eventually the club was obliged to fly in a specialist from Austria. The bloke in question was supposed to be some sort of top man in his field and as Olympiacos had a few players out with injury at the time, they must have got his services under some sort of job lot deal.

I'd already had enough so I phoned Freddie Griffiths (who had already saved my career once, when I was at Bury) at Manchester City and he arranged for me to get treated back in the UK. Olympiacos insisted, though, that I meet their Austrian specialist and so I met him at the airport before my flight home to the UK. We managed to get a consultation set up in some sort of private room at the airport and he pulled out a big needle, gave me a cortisone injection and I hobbled up the steps onto a plane bound for Manchester.

I was treated at Manchester City alongside one of their big stars, Colin Bell, who was also out with his infamous knee injury at that time. I remember the great cricketer Clive Lloyd was also there getting some treatment for a long-standing injury.

Both Freddie Griffiths and City treated me as one of their own. I could not have asked for better treatment. After Freddie gave me ultra-sound treatment to break up the swelling around my knee, he told me that I was going to have to work my nuts off to get the strength back in the thigh muscles that support the knee.

And that was how it played out: two weeks of intensive treatment and plenty of hard work to build up the muscle. On one occasion, Freddie worked me so hard that I crawled out of the gym on my hands and knees. Both Asa Hartford and Joe Corrigan were there to witness my humiliation, but I got no sympathy from Freddie, who just kicked me up the arse and called me a soft bastard.

But the regime was just what I needed, and I was fit again in a couple of weeks. God knows how long the process might have lasted in Greece. Neither Freddie nor Manchester City took a penny off me for this painfully effective treatment and I know that I will be forever indebted to them.

As soon as I was ready for action, I flew straight back to Greece where I scored four goals in consecutive games. Ludicrously, this didn't go down too well with everybody. There was a Greek international striker playing alongside me and I was making him look ordinary with my strike rate. It didn't help either that I stood out so much among the dark-haired Greeks with my shock of white-blond hair.

After a while the service to me from my team-mates dried up. They wouldn't even pass to me. If it hadn't been for my fellow foreigner, Sorensen, playing on the right wing, I would never have seen the ball. Sorensen was the sort who could put in a good cross from out wide on the wing and he did the best he could to end the campaign of isolation that I was enduring.

The Olympiacos coach at that time was a Serbian called Todor Veselinevic. He spoke no Greek and, as he didn't address me directly, I assumed he spoke no English either. He worked in tandem with an interpreter who translated all his tactics into Greek. Then there was another fella who could speak a bit of English and so he told me what the coach was saying.

Pleasingly, I was largely left to my own devices tactically. This suited me immensely as I liked to improvise in my own idiosyncratic fashion. Danny Blanchflower once said of me, "We don't know what he will do next so you can imagine what he does to the opposition."

We also frequently received team talks from the club president. Most of the time, the message was exactly the same: "The referee is well disposed towards us in this game, and if you go down in the box, you will definitely get a penalty!" I kid you not!

It didn't really take too long for the penny to drop and for me to realise that - at that time at least - the game was bent in Greece. We were nailed on certainties to win at home, as you knew that other teams would not be trying too hard away from home.

Naturally, when we played away from home, nobody was ever going to do us any favours. I remember one game we played away at Kastoria, up in the West Macedonian mountains. We played on a shale pitch, even though this was the top-flight of Greek football. It had taken a two-day journey by coach to get there but at least I got to see some of the off-the-beaten-track places that tourists to the country were never likely to see.

This game took place during the winter and there were no tourists there at all. I remember the setting as being by a beautiful lake. What was not so beautiful was the mood out on the pitch - the home team were kicking lumps off us.

Because of the distance involved, none of our own supporters had accompanied us on this odyssey, so when it all kicked-off we were completely alone. I remember one particular bloke who had deliberately stamped on my foot on two different occasions, so when play was at the other end of the pitch, I felled him with a right hander: that temper at work again.

Within two seconds just about every player on the opposing side had his hands round my throat trying to throttle me. I thought they were going to kill me. Somehow it all calmed down. I confess I don't quite understand what happened next. I wasn't officially sent off, but the coach strongly recommended that I come off the field of play and take a seat on the bench. Then they put the sub on. Only Olympiacos could get away with a stunt like that. That incident underlined the power of the club at that time.

The game re-started, and I was sitting on the bench cursing and screaming and vowing vengeance on the bloke who had kicked me. Until that moment I had been working under the impression that the coach spoke no English. He seemed pretty fluent, however, when he leant over and screamed full in my face, "Fucking shut up!"

Of course, there were good times too. Frances was there with me and we had a pretty good social life. One of my best friends in football, Les Shannon, who had previously had spells as manager of my former clubs Bury and Blackpool, was also out in Greece at that time having served as Olympiacos manager the previous season. Les was something of a legend in Greece, as he had achieved great things with PAOK of Salonika. He was there with his girlfriend, an English girl who was great with a lively, bubbly personality.

Les lived just five minutes away us, and we would go to his place and play cards. We also went out for the occasional meal in a restaurant with a couple of glasses of wine or maybe an ouzo, but it wasn't like the glamorous lifestyle that today's top footballers enjoy.

I loved Les and was devastated when I learned of his death in December 2007, long after his funeral had taken place. I was saddened to lose an old friend, a loss made greater by the fact that I had been unable to attend his funeral and pay him my respects.

Some of Les' stories merely served to confirm what I already knew; that football in Greece was corrupt. On one occasion he had even caught some of his colleagues dividing up the cash they had been paid to underperform. Les also told me about the corrupt way in which Olympiacos had always been run. Mind you, even I had finally cottoned on to that fact. When I wasn't being told to fall over in the box for a guaranteed penalty, I was occasionally being told not to score.

The first time I was ordered to shoot wide, I scored within ten minutes of kick-off, which didn't go down too well with my devoted colleagues. Nils Sorensen and I had decided to play by our own rules, which meant that we were both pariahs.

By this time, I was coming to the inevitable conclusion that I would not be staying in Greece. It was doing nothing for my international prospects, as Greek football got very little exposure outside Greece at that time. Even if I was playing well nobody knew back home in the UK. I didn't like the corruption and my team-mates were doing little to endear themselves to me. There was also the little matter of getting kicked to death every time I took to the pitch on our travels.

The following story gives some idea of the sense of isolation. After my performance against Holland in Rotterdam in October 1976, on the eve of my departure from Bury to Blackpool, I featured in an international versus West Germany in Cologne (I came on a substitute for Gerry Armstrong in a 5-0 defeat). I then earned my 12th cap against England in the Home Internationals, this time replacing Trevor Anderson when, despite a Chris McGrath goal, we were beaten 2-1.

Further appearances from the bench came against Scotland, Wales and a June fixture in Reykjavik against Iceland but that was my last cap before moving to Greece.

In the early part of the 1977/78 season I was apparently picked to play in a return game at home to Iceland in Belfast. Somehow, the telegram informing me that my services were wanted for the national team was sent not to Olympiacos but to Panathanaikos. So, even though it was incredibly unlikely that there were two Derek Spences playing in Athens at that time, it took so long for the telegram to cross the city that I didn't find out that I had made the team until two weeks after the game had taken place!

Of course, the Greeks cared nothing for my international career, but at least I can say that I still have that errant telegram to this day. That was to signal a 15-month absence from the Northern Ireland side that only served to increase my growing discontent. Given their tendency to bribe referees, it was hardly a surprise when Olympiacos found themselves in the Greek cup final that year. They were to face big, cross-town rivals AEK. In Britain such an important match would have been played at a neutral ground, but not in Greece.

AEK must have won the toss because we were to play the final at their home ground. This was in May and the temperatures were already far too high for football. When Olympiacos played at home the team normally stayed in a top-class hotel for a couple of nights before the game. As we were playing in Athens, we saw no reason to change our routine and we booked into a hotel.

At around one o'clock on the day of the big game we boarded a coach for the twenty-minute drive to AEK's ground. By this time it was sweltering. No sooner had we got on the bus than we were off it again. It had broken down and we were obliged to walk the rest of the way to the opposition's stadium. The streets around the stadium were thronged with AEK fans and we felt like sitting ducks as we made our way through them. Even an armed police escort didn't help our nerves. By the time we got there most of us were dripping with sweat and hardly in a fit state to play football.

Eventually, we arrived at the ground and went out onto the pitch to have a look around and soak up the atmosphere. It was complete bedlam: 45,000 AEK fans were taking the roof off with their partisan chanting. I think we had managed to attract a few fans, but far too few to dissipate the hostile atmosphere.

AEK were the top team in Greece at that time. We weren't too far behind and we could boast five Greek internationals in our starting line-up. We kicked off and within 15 minutes I had scored one of the best goals of my career. Somebody chipped the ball into the box and I took it with my back to the goal on the edge of the 18-yard box, swivelled and volleyed the ball as it came down: straight into the top corner! It was a complete fluke really, and one with some rather unusual consequences.

One of our supporters who was watching the game live on TV had a heart attack and died. I only hope he died a happy man! I know I was. We were on a £2,000 per man win bonus if we carried the day! So, there we were, 1 - 0 up in the final and in a great position. However, I was unaware that some of my colleagues had been offered an even bigger bung to lose.

The final score on that day was AEK 5 Olympiacos 1. By half-time I knew something was wrong. The only ones doing any running or making any kind of an effort were me, Sorensen and a little Argentinian player whose name escapes me now. We were working our nuts off but it was like the Alamo.

At half-time we were 3 - 1 down and I thought, naively, that we were still in with a chance. What I didn't know was that there was a clique of players who were unhappy with the coach Todor Veselinevic, and if they lost this big game that was a pretty good way of getting rid of their enemy. I might as well not have bothered scoring. With a bit of luck, the bloke that died might have gone to his resting place thinking we were well on the way to a resounding victory.

The next day we were all summoned to the team headquarters in Piraeus, which was housed in a big apartment complex where all the other Olympiacos teams had their base. Like Barcelona and Real Madrid, Olympiacos had all kinds of other sports teams associated with it: basketball, hockey, etc.

The president of the club stood in front of the assembled players and, one by one, he named and shamed those he knew to have taken a bribe. I remember there was a big centre half from the north of Greece who had not taken money. I was glad about that, because we had got on well and I wanted to retain my positive memories of him.

Quite rightly, although somewhat hypocritically, the club president was really throwing a wobbler. Via an interpreter I was told that he said, "On my tombstone it will say that I was the president when Olympiacos got beaten 5 – 1!" He was beside himself with rage and humiliation. He then went on to tell the ones who had taken the bribe that their tactic had misfired on them: he would get rid of them before the start of the next season. Coach Veselinevic and his backroom staff would be staying after all!

Todor Veselinevic, who died in 2017, was one of the most renowned goal-scorers in Yugoslavian football history. He played in the 1954 and 1958 World Cup finals, and during his coaching career led Fenerbahce to two Turkish League title triumphs, and Yugoslavia to the 1984 European Championship finals where his charges unfortunately lost all three games.

Todor was a good coach. His problem was that he had inherited a squad of players who had become accustomed to winning without trying. Olympiacos' previous owner, a shipping magnate called Basil Goulandris, had paid the opposition to lose in virtually every game. If he had been owner when I was there, I would have been a millionaire from all the winning bonuses he used to pay out whenever Olympiacos won. Olympiacos had been winning every game, which was not surprising when you consider the incentives offered to the opposition.

Interestingly, the name of Basil Goulandris, who died in 1984, has surfaced in the recent `Panama Papers' scandal. These documents reveal the extent to which some rich businessmen have used offshore companies to avoid domestic taxation.

One such ruse is to covertly move around billions of dollars-worth of art whilst attempting to minimise or completely avoid taxes in your homeland. Evidently, Goulandris spent many winter months in the Alpine resort of Gstaad with his wife Elise. The Greek couple amassed a billion-dollar art collection that they displayed in their chalet. A Greek heiress is now fighting a legal battle in Switzerland to find out what has become of a collection of Picasso, Van Gogh, Renoir, Monet, Cezanne and Degas art that she says should be part of her inheritance. So, who knows, if I'd have arrived in Greece earlier I might have acquired a famous work of art as a winning bonus!

Anyway, back to my story. I knew that the writing was on the wall in Greece after a relatively short space of time. Whilst the climate was great, and the lifestyle was free and easy, Greek football was something of an unknown quantity in Europe and I was beginning to feel isolated.

In January 1978 we found out that my wife, Frances, was pregnant with my eldest daughter, Leanna. A tragedy that happened to my little Argentinian teammate confirmed what we already knew: any child of ours was going to be born in the UK. The Argentinian lad had lost a baby under the most distressing of circumstances. His wife had delivered the baby and sometime afterwards, doctors came out of the delivery room and told him that the baby had died. Apparently if a baby was still born due to some abnormality, the local custom at the time was to get rid of the baby, as if there was some sort of shame attached to the event.

Frances and I were determined we were going to get the best care, both pre and post-natal. I had made good money and managed to save quite a bit of it, but I knew that with the corruption and everything else we were never really going to settle.

I loved much of life in Greece though and want to make it clear the local people were great with us. I adored the food, particularly moussaka and the delicious salads that are an important part of the diet there. I did get the worst bout of food poisoning ever whilst there but, never mind, overall the food was fantastic.

In Greek football back then they played a plethora of friendlies during a season. I scored a shed load of goals in the friendlies but only about six in competitive games, thanks mainly to the refusal of some colleagues to pass to me when I was in good goal-scoring positions.

It was in Greece too that I had my first chance encounter with my future nemesis Billy Bingham. He was managing a club in Cyprus back then, but he'd also worked in Greece and on one of his trips ashore I bumped into him. We shook hands and then out of the blue he asked me "Is your money okay?" Money was always a subject close to his heart. Bingham hated Les Shannon as they had managed rival clubs in Greece and I often wonder whether that affected his view of me.

I finally made the decision to come home in the immediate aftermath of the shambolic and shameful cup final. But Greek football had one last surprise waiting for me. In the very last game of the season I was told in no uncertain terms that I was not to score on that day. The 'right' result was either a nil-nil draw or a 0-1 home loss. A local team was going to beat us at home, something that was virtually unheard of, and to add insult to injury this local team was really not up to much.

By this time Nils Sorensen and I had had enough of the Greek attitude to football. Sorensen received the same instructions that I had been given: in other words, he was told to go missing. I suspected that Sorensen paid no attention to his briefing and I had my suspicions confirmed when, a few minutes into the game, he hit a sweet cross into me from his position over on the right wing. I knocked it in for the simplest of goals.

Not one of my team-mates cheered or congratulated me! That was how bad it was. The scenario on that day had been some sort of insurance policy for the next season. Our opponents needed a draw to stay up. If we furnished them with the right result, we would, in a quid-pro-quo agreement, be guaranteed two easy wins against them - both home and away - the following season.

Scoring that goal did nothing to make me popular with my team-mates, but by that time I didn't give a shit. I had already let the management know that I wanted to return to the UK and on a quick trip back home I was contacted by Arthur Cox, who was an up-and-coming manager at Chesterfield at that time. I agreed, in principle, to join Chesterfield upon my return home but in the end, that was not how things worked out.

Chapter 9 [1978-1980]
Back to Blackpool - Blackpool FC

Just before leaving Greece I received a phone call from Bob Stokoe, who had recently been appointed Blackpool manager. He wanted me to come back and have a second spell with the Seasiders. So, although I had given my word to Arthur Cox at Chesterfield, I decided to do what I thought was best for my family: I reneged on my promise and re-signed for Blackpool.

After learning of the missed telegram debacle, my international career with Northern Ireland resumed. Danny Blanchflower was still at the helm and I returned to the fold immediately.

My daughter, Leanna, was born 18 September 1978. Just before her birth I had been recalled to the Northern Ireland squad for a derby fixture in Dublin against the Republic of Ireland. I was due to meet Jimmy Nichol, Sammy McIlroy, David McCreary and one or two others, who had hired their own light aircraft to fly from Manchester to Dublin.

As I was set to leave the house, Frances informed me that her waters had broken and that she needed an ambulance. Back then there was no way you could pull out of a football match even for the birth of your first child. I had been in the international wilderness whilst in Greece and this was not just any old game either, it being an historic first meeting of the two Irish countries on a football field. If I pulled out of what was to be my first game for my country in 15 month's I knew my international career would probably be over.

To my shame, I left the house and Frances was compelled to cope on her own. I can't help but feel that my attitude of always putting football ahead of our domestic arrangements was at the heart of our subsequent break-up. I don't think our relationship ever recovered from my decision that day.

Looking back, I let Frances down and if I could have my time over again I'd have put my family first, but that is with the benefit of hindsight and, as I have said, back then it wasn't the done thing. Any refusal to join up with the squad would have been interpreted as disloyalty on my part. In 1978 fathers weren't necessarily expected to be at the birth and many men went to work and visited their wife and new offspring in hospital on the way home. Looked at now, my behaviour appears uncaring and I sensed that even though attitudes in general were different then, Frances never forgave me and my already rocky relationship with her parents deteriorated beyond recovery.

The game between the two Irish national teams was played at the height of 'The Troubles'. It was no ordinary game of football. Tensions were running high, but in the end the match turned out to be a highly unmemorable 0-0 draw, which was played out against a general backdrop of peace and harmony. There was certainly no significant trouble at the game.

The start of the 1978/79 season saw me playing for Blackpool again. I signed a two-year contract in July 1978 and was on a basic wage of £150 a week.

Blackpool had just been relegated to the old third division, which came as a bit of a shock for a club with such a distinguished history, although worse was to follow after I left again two years later when they ended up in the fourth division, even suffering the ignominy of seeking re-election in 1983.

The previous season Blackpool had sacked my old mentor Allan Brown in controversial circumstances, with Jimmy Meadows taking over on a caretaker basis. The seasiders went on a horrific run, sliding from a position just outside the promotion places to 20th. Cardiff City, who had previously looked doomed, stayed up and Blackpool were down to the third tier. A far cry from the halcyon days of Matthews and Mortenson.

Bob Stokoe had taken over the managerial reins and was already in the process of building a decent squad of players when I signed on the dotted line.

The move to Blackpool also meant that I could hang on to my nice house in Preesall: something I would never have been able to do if I had gone to Chesterfield. I felt I had unfinished business at Bloomfield Road, viewing that I had yet to prove myself for Blackpool. During Allan Brown's time at the club, the system they played never suited me and I thought I could do a better job for them with their new shape. Naturally, it had been a great experience for me to play alongside such great strikers as Micky Walsh and Bob Hatton, but for this second stint I was to be the main striker. A prospect I relished.

A lad called Mel Holden, who had been at Sunderland, was to be my partner. He was big and strong, and in the pre-season training games we seemed to reach an understanding.

There was something of a clique of players who, along with Bob Stokoe, had a Sunderland connection. Bobby Kerr, who had captained the Black Cats during their famous 1973 FA Cup final victory over Leeds United, was in the team at the time, as was Dick Malone, who had also played in Sunderland's giant-killing cup team.

Kerr was now the captain at Blackpool and I remember he had to finish football when he suffered a bizarre injury: he accidentally trod on the ball and threw his hip out. Despite being treated for six months at the specialist Wrightington Hospital near Wigan (a well-known venue for all northern footballers at that time), they could do nothing for him and this freak accident finished his career.

Blackpool had been widely expected to bounce straight back up to the second division, but the fact is that we did not get off to a good start to the season.

Mel Holden was struggling. He seemed to be getting slower with every match and the fans really got on his back. Blackpool sold him to a Dutch club and almost immediately thereafter he was diagnosed with multiple sclerosis and was dead within six months of his move to Holland. This came as a great shock to all of us, as he was still in his 20's when he died.

To fill the gap left by Mel Holden, Blackpool bought Tony Kellow from Exeter to play up front alongside me. Tony was a great little goal scorer and a smashing bloke. I remember having a few nights out with him at a local pub called Wardley's Creek. Tony too, died prematurely when he succumbed to kidney failure at the age of 58.

There was no doubt that my spell in Greece had improved me as a player. I was a lot more skilful and I thought that I had benefited from Greek training methods. Even though some of the things about Greek football at that time were quite primitive, like playing on shale pitches, in many ways their training was ahead of ours. Pre-match meals would consist of pasta, whereas in the UK, most players were stilling eating a big steak a couple of hours before kick-off.

Much of the training in Greece was based on ball skills, rather than on pure fitness work, so all in all I considered myself to be a more rounded professional than in my previous spell at Blackpool and wanted to use these newly acquired skills and do a really good job for the club.

And I did do well for the Pool. I was leading goal-scorer and I also won the coveted "Player of The Year" trophy, something that means a lot to all professional footballers.

By this time Micky Walsh was long gone and the team had a makeshift quality about it. Although my great mate Terry Pashley was now starring at left back after the departure of Steve Harrison, but we seemed to lack any degree of organisation on the pitch.

Despite our faults, we managed a few good results, like when we beat Ipswich Town 2-0 at Bloomfield road in a cup game. And this at a time when the Tractor Boys were a first division outfit and one of the best sides around. We also drew with Manchester City at home in another cup tie, a game in which I scored.

At Christmas of that year, I scored two goals in a 3-0 win over Chester City. That game featured on ITV's Kick-Off programme. I particularly remember that, because after the match we were celebrating our win in Blackpool's Tangerine Club and Bob Stokoe was given a rousing reception. Then, out of the blue, he was given the dreaded vote of confidence by the board of directors. All football fans know what happens after that and Bob was no exception to the rule: he was sacked the following week.

I can still remember the scene, when he brought all the players together in the little dressing room under the old South Stand at Bloomfield Road. To say he was upset would be the understatement of the century. He described the board as the biggest bunch of crooks he had ever come across in football. He was absolutely fuming. Don't forget that at the time, Bob Stokoe was still a big name in football. It was only five years since he had led Sunderland to their giant killing moment of glory against the mighty Leeds United. Bob spelt it out in no uncertain terms that he thought the club was being run by a shower of buffoons. Or words to that effect.

I owe a debt to Bob. I had been getting clobbered with predictable regularity by some of the division's more notorious enforcers. I had, however, struggled to turn the other cheek and had picked up quite a few bookings for retaliation. Stokoe called me into his office and told me that he was dropping me for my poor disciplinary record. To add insult to injury, he fined me a week's wages.

I was absolutely livid, as I was leading goal-scorer at the time and running myself into the ground week in week out. But he was right about the discipline. A week out gave me time to think and I don't think I was ever booked for dissent again. I appreciated his honesty and his habit of conducting business on a face to face basis.

I was now a regular again with the Northern Ireland squad, scoring the equaliser in an October 1978 win against Denmark in Belfast. Most of my family were there, even Mummy left the kitchen for a few hours to share my moment. One sour note though was the Danish goalkeeper landing heavily on me after a collision and trapping a nerve in my leg. An injury that niggled me for quite some time.

But despite my success on the international front, things were about to get a bit strange at Blackpool. A chap by the name of Peter Lawson, who was a local solicitor, had made a bid to become the club chairman. I got a phone call from somebody in the press asking me if it was true that he had the backing of the players in this power struggle.

I refused to make any comment, as I have always been of the belief that a footballer's job is simply to do their best and leave the off-field machinations to those involved in running the football club. I certainly did not see it as being my role to get involved in selecting the club chairman. I had nothing against Peter Lawson personally and was neither for nor against his candidacy.

While this was going on, some of the Sunderland lads were going around with a clipboard and asking people to sign a petition backing Stan Ternent for the vacant manager's slot. They approached me on the training ground and asked me to sign. Much to their obvious chagrin, I refused.

I still think today that the selection of managers and directors is best left out of the players' hands, but I was also concerned that if Stan Ternent was appointed manager and the team then went on a losing run, would some of the fallout come down on the players? Stan had been Bob Stokoe's assistant, but even so it was not my business to decide who should succeed Bob.

In the end, Peter Lawson was appointed director and Stan Ternent took on the managerial role, and for a while all was well.

That said, Blackpool finishing the season in 12th was a disaster, and it was made clear that the following campaign would need to be a massive improvement. On a personal note, I scored 16 goals, including a hat-trick at home to Carlisle United, and I'd reclaimed my place in the Northern Ireland set up, so I certainly couldn't grumble.

Right at the start of the 1979/80 season, in fact in the first match, I got injured again. We were playing at Grimsby and a fella by the name of Bobby Cummings went right over the top and really did me. I heard later that he told at least one of my team-mates that he and I had 'history'! This came as news to me, as I had never heard of him. History or not, I had obviously upset him somehow, judging by the way he came in with both feet and took me out at the knee. A challenge like that could have finished my career and I was pleased to see that in subsequent matches in which he featured my team-mates made it a point of honour to avenge me and kick shit out of the bastard.

In the end there were no broken bones and with treatment from Alan Smith - the Blackpool physio who went on to work with Arsenal and the English national team - I was back playing again by October. I went straight back into the first team, although the reality was that I was nowhere near match fit. In-fact I was way off the pace.

And that was basically that. By December 1979, I'd left for a new club and once again my time at Blackpool had been far shorter than I'd wanted.

One wonderful aspect of my second spell with Blackpool was meeting an up-and-coming midfielder by the name of Wayne Harrison. He was a lovely lad and we soon became pals. When I left for Southend, as is often the case in football when you leave one club for another, we didn't stay in touch, but many years later our paths would cross once more and not only would we again work together but he would also become a long-standing and much-loved friend.

Chapter 10 [1979-1982]
Into the unknown - Southend United

The call from Southend came out of the blue. I knew that, because I had been playing whilst not quite match fit, my form had dipped but, that aside, I thought that things were pretty settled at Blackpool.

I had sold my little house in Preesall and moved into a bigger one in a little village called Hambleton, which is about seven miles away from Blackpool, on the far side of the River Wyre; in an area all the locals call Over Wyre: so the last thing I wanted was another move.

I went to see Stan Ternent and told him I was quite shocked at the thought of a move down south. The boss then told me that it was pretty much a done deal, I would be going to Southend United and one of their players, Colin Morris would be heading north in a swap deal. I told the boss that I didn't even know where Southend was and I certainly had no interest in playing there. Stan told me that if I didn't agree to the deal, the alternative was to freeze my arse off all season on the subs' bench. Ironically, he was sacked in February 1980 anyway, so it was his backside that ended up colder than mine.

The day after this bombshell I drove down to Northampton, where for some reason, all the interested parties had elected to do business. At this time Blackpool were mid-table and Southend were at the bottom of the third division.

Peter Lawson drove me down to Northampton in his Mercedes. Perhaps this new move was all about my refusal to support his bid for the chairmanship and the Sunderland mafia's attempts to get Ternent appointed.

Southend's manager at that time was Dave Smith who asked me what sort of terms I was willing to accept. I pulled a figure out of the air - £240 a week and a signing on fee of £15,000. These figures came straight off the top of my head; this was long before the days of football agents representing players.

I did not want to go to Southend and thought that my exorbitant demands would somehow save me from a trip to the south coast. Dave Smith left the room, probably to have a word with his chairman on the phone, and when he came back in he agreed to my terms. You could have knocked me down with a feather. And the contract was for two and a half years; the most security I'd ever been offered.

Despite my initial reluctance to complete the deal, I took some comfort from the fact that at £100,000 I was Southend's most expensive signing to date (despite my pleasure at being a record breaker, no actual money changed hands in this deal as Colin Morris was also valued at £100,000).

Whilst Frances absorbed the news that she was set to move home yet again, I went down on my own to Southend by train, leaving my car at home, and was put up by the club in a hotel until more suitable accommodation could be found. My debut came away at Rotherham, followed by another away game at, of all places, Bloomfield Road.

Southend used to play most of their home games on a Friday night - something to do with not wanting to compete with the big London clubs, West Ham United in particular. This tactic worked for them and they got some pretty big gates. I used to like playing in those Friday night games, perhaps because I scored on my home debut in a 3-0 win against Hull City.

Although I hadn't wanted to relocate again, Southend turned out to be a good move for me, not least for the fact that Frances and I found out we were expecting our second child.

I was on good wages and after a spell in a hotel, paid for by the club, I moved into a house owned by the club, for which I paid no rent.

Keith Mercer was signed to play up front with me and we made a pretty effective striking partnership.

Southend United were a good team. There were no prima donnas and there was a good sense of equality and camaraderie.

They were well-organised, and everybody was prepared to work. What they did lack though was a bit of luck. Sometimes in football, things just won't run for you, and that was what happened at Southend that season.

We went into the last game of the season, away at Hull City, needing a draw to stay up. We played Hull off the park, but it is goals that count when you are looking at the record books. They won 1-0 and we were relegated to the fourth division.

That was the first time I had ever suffered the ignominy of relegation and it was made all the more bitter by the fact that it happened in Hull, where my sister-in-law lived.

In all, I scored five goals that campaign; a reasonable enough tally in a struggling side.

Obviously, the next season (1980/81) was all about whether or not we could fight our way out of the bottom tier of English league football.

After my initial doubts, I settled in well. It was nice to live a house belonging to the club, and it was beneficial from a financial point of view. It also seemed that it was always that bit warmer down on the south coast than it was in Blackpool.

Another big turning point for me was the opportunity to rekindle a friendship I had made in Bury, through good friends Gary and Anne Clarke, who were massive Bury supporters.

Alf Whelan was a friend of Gary's dad, who originated from Manchester but who had relocated to Southend to work for the Ford Motor Company. Alf and his wife Aud made Francis and I so welcome and we became very close, so much so that he became almost like a second father to me. Alf and I were inseparable, and we spent most of our free time together. This friendship continued well after my retirement from football, with Alf and myself regularly going away together on holiday. He had a wicked, dry sense of humour, which I loved, and I have countless memories of us howling around in laughter at the silliest of things.

Alf passed in the year 2000, I remember getting the phone call early one morning from his son whilst I was sat in one of my flats at Fleetwood. I was inconsolable as it was such a shock, he hadn't been ill, he just died in his sleep, which was exactly the way he would have wanted to go. I still miss him to this day, but I cherish the memories of all the good times we spent laughing and joking during our wonderful friendship.

The team found themselves in the position of being heavy favourites to go straight back up to the third division. In the end that was exactly what happened. We won the fourth division title at a canter and went back up as champions.

Our son Matthew had been born in January 1981 and I couldn't have been happier with life.

During our headlong charge for promotion, we broke just about every record for the club. It was hardly surprising then, that I found myself enjoying my football like never before.

The team tended to socialise together, so there was a great atmosphere and a buzz about the place. I was scoring goals for fun: leading goal-scorer (21 from 49 appearances) and Player of the Year. That was a title I had now won twice. I also had a fourth division champions' medal, my first real honour in club football.

Southend had a history of being a bit of a yo-yo club, going up and down through the divisions, but they had never won any divisional title until that season. We finished two points clear of Lincoln City and were unbeaten at home. The title was secured with one game still remaining when we travelled to Torquay and won 3-0. I was even chaired off the pitch at the end by our ecstatic fans. The promotion party took place the following weekend when Rochdale held us to a 1-1 draw at Roots Hall in front of 10,668 spectators.

One personal highlight was a hat-trick versus York City in September. I recall the fans chanting 'Derek Spence is an international'.

During that championship winning season, we had a fantastic team with a mix of experience and youth. Two of the younger lads were Danny Greaves and Garry Nelson and I like to think that I had a hand in helping them along their way. I remember meeting Danny for the very first time, not least because his dad was my childhood hero. Before I even realised who he was I had given him the sound advice to take his hands out of his tracky-bottoms as the gaffer would have gone off his head at him. It was only after our little chat that someone informed me that he was Jimmy's son.

Danny signed professional terms in 1981 and I was delighted for him. Years later I was absolutely thrilled to be asked back down to Roots Hall to play in his testimonial when I also spent a wonderful couple of hours in the company of the great man himself Jimmy Greaves. Danny and I remain friends to this day.

Garry was a breath of fresh air, the team before his arrival was starting to go a little bit stale, maybe a little bit predictable. He just gave us an added dimension as a wide player, with fantastic pace and an eye for a goal. As well as being a top player he also had a great personality and got on with everyone in the team, a real all-round team player. It was no surprise that he went on to have a great career at Charlton.

My striking partner up front was Keith Mercer and it was undoubtedly the best striking partnership that I have ever played in. We complemented each other's games, Merce could hold the ball up well as he was so strong, and he was a lethal finisher in front of goal. The one thing though about him that used to drive me mad was his incessant snoring which kept me awake when we roomed together, and I would inevitably end up having to take a sleeping tablet just to get off to sleep. Merce is still one of my closest friends in football and we speak regularly, however his move down to St Albans means we don't see as much of each other now.

Two of the more experienced players of that team were Alan Moody and Ronnie Pountney, who were both seasoned pros and we're undoubtedly the steadying influence if the lads were getting a bit nervy. Ronnie may have been small in stature but was a ferocious competitor in every game he played, whereas Alan was as cool as a cucumber and never lost his composure, both players showing the younger players how it should be done.

I got on well with the fans and really enjoyed my football. It was also a source of some pride for me that I was picked, by the PFA, to be in the representative side for the Division Four. This was ahead of my old mate, Mick Hartford, who was top scorer with Lincoln at the time and who even went on to play for England during his time at Luton Town.

At all the teams I've played at I felt it important to mix with the supporters who would turn up week in week out to support their team rain or shine.

One such supporter from Southend was a gentleman called Dave Brabbing who I remember presenting me with a trophy to mark my 100th goal, that he had made himself, listing all the goals I had scored during my career. Dave is all that is good about football supporters, passionate about his club, respectful of other clubs and supporters, and just a generally nice guy who I was very fortunate to meet.

One of the off-field things that gave me the greatest pleasure was the involvement we players had in charity work. One of the beneficiaries of our work was a local youngster called Tony Herring, who needed a kidney transplant. The whole team got behind him and raised money for his treatment.

All in all it was a fantastic time and I treasure those memories to this very day.

Chapter 11 [1980]

Other side of the world for 20 minutes - Northern Ireland on tour in Australia

In 1980, Billy Bingham took over as Northern Ireland manager for the second time and although I didn't know it at the time, that was the beginning of the end of my days as an international footballer.

I had been sad to see Danny Blanchflower leave. As mentioned earlier, he was a bit of a football snob and undoubtedly looked down at players like me who plied their trades in the lower leagues, but I still loved him, probably because his eccentricities made me laugh so much.

He had some funny ideas did Danny. In training, he used to have us working on defending free kicks just outside the box by retreating 15 yards rather than the mandatory ten. This cunning ploy was to help the goalkeeper apparently by giving him more time to see the ball in flight!

Another cunning ruse was for us to employ low throw in techniques (no, me neither!), whilst my personal favourite was the sessions he put on where he instructed us to dribble with two balls rather than just the one. Apparently, if you could master two balls at a time, control of just the one ball in match time would become a piece of piss!

Because of his innate snobbery and my lower league status, Danny invariably answered any query raised by me with the retort "Derek hasn't grasped it." No shit Sherlock. Nor have your first division stars.

One less attractive aspect of our relationship though was his penchant for referring to me by a nickname that, mercifully, only he adopted. Danny's chosen sobriquet was "Gusty Spence". Not too bad I suppose, no worse than Snowball even, until you learned that Gusty Spence was a leader of the paramilitary Ulster Volunteer Force (UVF). I still recall with horror him introducing me to Martin O'Neill - a passionate Irish nationalist and, in later life, manager of the Republic of Ireland national team - with the words: "Martin, let me introduce you to Gusty Spence". Fair play to Martin, he just giggled and shook my hand.

Danny even referred to me as Gusty Spence when talking to the press/media about me and so, as you can imagine, I dreaded my name ever cropping up during press conferences which involved the input of my boss, especially if Gusty and the UVF were headline news at that time.

To be fair to Gusty, though, after being released from prison in 1984 he became a community worker in the Shankhill Road area. In later life, after joining the Progressive Unity Party (PUP), he emerged as an important political figure in the peace process, participating in negotiations and announcing the Loyalist ceasefire in October 1994 which was one of the key steps towards normality which culminated in the 1998 Good Friday agreement. Spence died in Belfast in September 2011, aged 78, and at his request, he was buried without Loyalist paramilitary honours or trappings.

Bingham's first overseas trip as Northern Ireland boss was to Australia, where the team was due to play four games at different venues: Sydney, Melbourne, Adelaide and Perth. That is quite a daunting workload for a two-week trip, especially when you consider the jetlag and acclimatisation. It seemed that, when we weren't playing football, we were either in the air or booking into yet another hotel.

We flew out on a jumbo jet and I was in the middle aisle along with Martin O'Neill, Jimmy Nicholl and Tommy Cassidy. We were all playing three-card brag. It was ludicrous to think that I could gamble on even terms in such illustrious company. They were all earning fortunes in the old first division, whilst I was on third division wages. I lost £350 quid in the first hour and effectively blew my spending money for the tour. After that I never gambled again. I never had many vices thankfully.

During a little break from our card school the expenses sheet was passed around. Naturally, I saw that as an opportunity to claw back some of my losses. All the lads were at it, claiming for things like, "Taxi to the airport" and so on. So I joined in the fun too; claiming for taxis here, there and everywhere. I remember I was listening to some music on my headphones at the time, which made it a bit easier for the lads to set me up for what was to come.

Tommy Cassidy leaned over my shoulder and said, "You'll never get away with that, Spencey. Billy won't wear it!" To which I replied, "Ah fuck him!" This was exactly the result the lads had been hoping for: Billy Bingham was standing looking over my other shoulder!

Consequently, you could say that ours was a doomed relationship right from the start. And from then on, it only got worse.

Eventually, we arrived in Sydney after a 27-hour flight and naturally, we were all knackered. When it came time for the boss to allocate rooms, I was expecting to be rooming with Jimmy Nicholl, which I had always done when on international duty. Billy Bingham obviously had other plans and informed me that I would be sharing a room with a bloke called Colin McCurdy, who I had never even heard of. I had never met him and all I knew about him was that he played for Linfield, oh, and there was just one other little detail: he had just been released from the notorious Long Kesh (Maze) Prison!

Colin and a few other lads from the Irish league had been brought on the trip, the idea being that it was a great way of showcasing their skills. Naturally, if some of them caught the eye of a scout for some big club and got a move as a result of the trip, then Billy Bingham would no doubt put himself in line for some sort of fee.

I was disappointed not to be rooming with Jimmy, but it was not the end of the world. The manager's word is final on such matters. In the end, Colin and I became great mates and I benefited greatly from his long, instructional talks on how to make a Molotov cocktail and how to strip down a sniper's rifle. But, seriously, I loved Colin to bits and we ended up getting on really well.

There was a bloke on tour with us who was a sort of a self-trained physiotherapist, a bloke by the name of Bobby McGregor, who was famous in Ireland for his "healing hands." These days such a position would require a string of qualifications as long as your arm, but those were simpler times.

It was from Bobby that I heard why things were never going to be good between me and Billy Bingham. He pulled me to one side in Melbourne and told me that the manager thought I was a bit of a "raker" - Northern Irish slang for a dickhead. I told Bobby that I thought I was no different to any of the other lads.

Jimmy Nicholl and I were always at the heart of any craic that was going on, especially when I used to do my famous impersonation of Danny Blanchflower, so maybe it was that what set Bingham against me, but I was certain there must have been more to it than me liking a laugh.

We had our first game - against the Australian national side - very early on in the tour. We played them in Sydney and beat them 2-0. I managed to get on the pitch for the last 20 minutes of what had been a pretty good performance.

The footballing side of things was clearly off to a good start, but we were not able to enjoy Sydney's famous tourist hotspots, Bondi Beach, the Sydney Opera House, Sydney Harbour Bridge. All of these things remained a mystery to us. All we saw was the notorious King's Cross, red light area, where some of the lads took full advantage of the many and varied entertainments on offer. Not me though of course. No vices as I said previously.

From Sydney it was on to Melbourne; Australia's second city and according to some, (due to the huge number of Greek immigrants) the second biggest Greek city in the world. I was really looking forward to playing in Melbourne as I knew that a lot of the Greek population knew me from my time with Olympiacos.

If some of the locals did want to see me play, they were going to be disappointed. I sat on the bench all night and never got a look in. Most of the subs got on the pitch and it was now beginning to sink in that the boss really did have a very low opinion of me. Some of this might have stemmed from my time in Greece. Billy Bingham was manager of PAOK when I was there and he knew of my close friendship with Les Shannon, who was his great rival in Greece.

If the football was going badly for me, at least I had a chance to enjoy Australian hospitality. While we were in Melbourne we had our photos taken with a local Aussie rules football team. Victoria is the heartland of their version of footie and we were treated fantastically well everywhere we went and made to feel very welcome.

Our third game was to be in Adelaide and when we arrived in the city, the local Irish community held a function for us. This invitation came from the nationalist side of the great divide in Irish society, but again, we were made to feel right at home and the political situation back home was never an issue.

In Adelaide I never got on the pitch and was feeling increasingly frustrated. My last hopes for a game rested on our final destination, Perth. With all the flying and the moving from hotel to hotel, a lot of us were pretty knackered most of the time. I remember Jimmy Nicholl and I had our photo taken with matchsticks propping our eyelids open, which was our way of letting people know how gruelling the schedule was. On one occasion, Colin and I overslept - possibly as a result of a late night - and Billy Bingham had to ring our room in order to rouse us from our slumbers.

On arriving in Perth we were welcomed by the loyalist side of the great Irish Diaspora and once again nobody was made to feel uncomfortable. The political situation back home was not mentioned, although naturally, there was some politics in the fact that we had attended one essentially Catholic shindig in Adelaide and one essentially Protestant bash in Perth.

In Sydney, we had played against the full national team, but due to the cost and the logistics of flying their team around the country, the rest of our games were played against a selection of the best, locally based players. In Perth, we were up against a particularly weakened version of the national side.

Needless to say, all the subs got a run out except me. I was fuming but I didn't want confrontation. I don't like arguing with people and knew it would do my cause no good having a stand-up row with the boss. He was the manager and he was clearly marking out his territory. The rest of the lads encouraged me to have it out with him, but my attitude was, "Fuck him!" To take somebody on such a long trip and only give them 20 minutes of football looked like a strange decision then and still looks that way now almost 40 years later.

I knew that Billy Bingham thought that I was a bit of a raker, but I wasn't any different from anybody else. For some reason, if we did stay out a bit too late, it always seemed to be me that got caught sneaking back into the team hotel in the wee small hours of the morning. Many top modern footballers are obsessive about diet, nutrition and rest and nowadays, there would be a strict curfew in place, but those were less sophisticated times and some high jinks was not only tolerated but expected.

In Australia, Bingham wanted a £50 fee for every little interview. Every time we stepped off a plane, local TV crews would ask for a word and they would be directed to David Bowen, the new head of the Irish FA, who would be left to broker these embarrassing little deals. Nobody had ever thought to charge for these things previously. That is how he got the nickname, 'Fifa Billy' (a fee for this and fee for that). He even had his own separate expense account, so that his demands could be kept apart from those of the players.

When he was in Spain with the World Cup squad in 1982, he had the habit of selling all the promotional freebies that he had been given; even trying to sell the lads the designer sunglasses that some company had given him. "Here you are, lads. You will need these, you know!" was his cry as he hawked his surplus freebies.

Chapter 12 [1981-1982]

World Cup heartache - Teletext and Billy Bingham

Naturally with me, when things are going well, that can only mean one thing: that an injury is waiting for me around the corner.

It happened in my second full season with Southend (1981-82). I went up for a header with my usual blind disregard for my own safety and I clashed heads with a defender, I was knocked out cold. The next thing I knew was waking up in hospital with concussion.

I couldn't play for a couple of weeks and whilst I was convalescing the directors asked me to make a presentation to a chap who had been some sort of long-serving commissionaire with the club. The poor fella was in the same hospital as me with chicken pox. I was reassured that he was long past the contagious stage of the disease, but it turned out that I was misinformed. My little act of goodwill got me a nasty dose of shingles for my troubles. That illness was to cost me dearly.

Southend ended the 1981/82 season in a respectable seventh position. I finished third top scorer with just eight goals, Keith Mercer and Steve Phillips outscoring me in an injury and illness hit season for yours truly.

The bout of shingles happened during the run-in to the 1982 World Cup in Spain. With hindsight, I think that spell of illness took more away from my game than I realised at the time. It is a nasty malady, but I didn't grasp just how long-lasting the effects would be.

It took a while to recover and get back to fitness, but even when I reclaimed my place in the Shrimper's squad I felt drained of energy and for someone like me this was a disaster as a major part of my game was work-rate, chasing lost causes and generally running hard for 90 minutes.

The shingles undoubtedly diminished my effectiveness, although at the time I just got on with it, as you do. I reasoned that I only needed a run of games to get back to my best. These days I would have been looked after much better but back then you were nothing to the manager if unavailable for action and were therefore desperate to play on regardless of the cost to you personally.

Some people think that my shingles-induced lack of form might have influenced Billy Bingham's subsequent decision regarding his World Cup squad, but I very much doubt that. To the best of my knowledge he watched me just once during that period.

I had played in four of the six qualifying games and was naturally hoping to make it all the way to the finals. By this time I had been a member of the Northern Ireland team for seven seasons and the manager, Billy Bingham, had been in the job for two years.

As part of the build up to Spain '82, Northern Ireland played a warm-up game in Paris at the Parc des Princes stadium in March. We were defeated 4-0 and I managed to get on as a sub, replacing Sammy McIlroy. Billy Caskey and Ian Stewart also made fleeting appearances from the bench, coming on for Terry Cochrane and David McCreery, so I was in good company.

I had one good chance and was only denied a goal when my header was cleared off the line, so although mine had not been a stellar performance, I still thought there was a good chance I would be going to Spain. Indeed, I could not see any reason for Bingham to leave me out. Although I never started a game for him - something I little reflected on at the time but now realise was probably very significant - I had been a regular throughout his reign and had worked my arse off in games and training trying to impress him. Despite not starting for him, I never refused a call up, even travelling to Australia for just 20 minutes of game time, so my commitment to the cause was obvious.

At the airport on the way out of Paris, I shook hands with Billy Bingham and he said, "I'll see you in May." This I took to be confirmation that I would indeed be going to the World Cup. The great Pat Jennings knew that I had supported Spurs as a boy and kindly gave me a pair of his goalkeeping gloves as a souvenir. Little did I know at the time that this would effectively be a leaving present and that there would be no more appearances in a Northern Ireland shirt for me! There appeared to be three strikers competing for a place in the starting line-up. Or at least that was what I thought at the time.

Billy Hamilton, Gerry Armstrong and I had been international colleagues for some time but the problem for us was that many critics perceived us to be similar in our playing styles. Consequently, we all felt insecure about our places in the pecking order and were equally desperate to not only assure ourselves of a place in the squad but also a place in the starting line-up.

I got the chance to show that I still had something to offer in comparison to one of my rivals when on 20 April 1982, with the World Cup squad set to be announced in just a matter of days, Southend - back in the third division by now of course - played Billy Hamilton's Burnley. With Bingham watching from the stands, Southend were soon down to ten men as Dave Cusack got sent off early in the first half, but I scored two second half goals in an astonishing 5-3 victory against a Burnley side that romped the league that year.

Burnley, containing stars such as a then youthful Trevor Steven and Republic of Ireland international Paul McGee, threw everything forward, hoping that their numerical advantage would work for them, but every time their attacks broke down, we would hit them on the break.

Naturally, after such a display I imagined that I was a stick-on to be picked for the next squad, only to learn later that Billy Bingham had left at halftime and therefore not witnessed my second half exploits.

The squad for the Home International series and the World Cup was announced at the end of the 1982 domestic football season. Despite my heroics against Burnley, I had been going through a sticky patch with Southend and there had been talk of my moving on. I was by now 30 years old and my contract was up. Manager, Dave Smith, for reasons that I couldn't fathom, had started to blank me and there was no suggestion of a new deal coming my way.

These days, if a manager was to treat a player in that fashion, they or their agent would challenge the manager and demand an explanation, but back then players didn't have freedom of contract and we certainly didn't have agents so you simply accepted the treatment doled out to you, hoping that a new contract offer would eventually materialise. Usually, a player got the silent treatment when the boss wanted you out, so naturally I was unsettled and increasingly concerned about my immediate future.

But I was still confident of getting to Spain, as the final squad would consist of 22 players and I had already been a member of a preliminary squad.

When it was time to announce the squad, Billy Bingham didn't contact me, so I learned my fate on Teletext. I looked at the TV screen and began reading down the list and, as I scanned the names, I began to get a sinking feeling in the pit of my stomach. When I got to the bottom of the list, my worst fears were confirmed. My name was not there. I would not be going to the World Cup.

To add insult to injury, there were four players - from the Irish league - I had never heard of. I had been a member of the national team for seven years and now I was out in the cold, with no explanation.

Bingham's first game in charge had been a friendly with Israel in March 1980. I was a second-half sub in place of Tom Finney in a dull goalless draw. That had set the pattern.

I didn't get a look in during the May Home International series which Northern Ireland won thanks to victories over Scotland and Wales and a draw with England at Wembley. Then came the aforementioned Australian tour.

My next opportunity arose in March 1981 when I was a second-half replacement for Billy Hamilton in a 1-1 draw at Hampden Park versus Scotland. In June I again came on for Hamilton during a 1-0 defeat to Sweden in Stockholm and my only other appearance for Bingham - and ultimately my last for my country - was the Paris game in March 1982.

So just four substitute outings in two years but still I maintained the belief that I was a part of Bingham's plans. Certainly, any fears I may have had about my immediate international career had been eliminated by that handshake at Paris airport.

Over the years, many people have assumed that the inclusion of the uncapped 17-year-old Norman Whiteside was why I missed out. However, this is not the case. If anything, it was the call up of Bobby Campbell that destroyed my dream. Bobby, who sadly died aged just 60 in 2016, was called up following a public campaign to lift a life ban imposed by the Irish FA following an incident involving a crash in a stolen car whilst he was on youth team duty in Switzerland in 1975.

Bobby, a colourful character throughout his career, had enjoyed a prolific season with Bradford City and eventually the IFA succumbed, and Bobby won his only two caps during the Home Internationals. He then took his place on the plane to Spain for the World Cup, during which he failed to make an appearance. Had he played a part in the tournament I think my bitterness over the decision to ignore me would have been assuaged somewhat, but the fact that Bobby saw as much action as I did back home in Hambleton made matters worse.

But for the clamour to select Bobby, I strongly believe that I would have gone to Spain for the World Cup. Norman's emergence didn't affect my chances at all and of course he went on to become a major star, playing in all of Northern Ireland's games during Spain '82. Not that I watched any of it. I was so devastated by my omission that I couldn't bring myself to view any of the games, never mind those involving my fellow countrymen.

Indeed, until discussing this chapter with Paul Cambridge, I wasn't even aware that my old team-mate Mal Donaghy had been sent off in the famous 1-0 victory over Spain in Valencia. Proof if any were needed as to how little notice I paid to that competition, such was my pain.

To be honest, had I not cut myself off from it completely the mental anguish would have made me ill. Even today, 37 long years later, the memory of my exclusion still causes me severe heartache. Indeed, it has only been since Jimmy Nicholl's appointment as assistant to current manager Michael O'Neill that I have re-discovered an interest in the national team. Jimmy kindly invited me to a couple of games and I'm now a keen fan again, but it took more than three decades before I could find anything remotely close to closure over World Cup '82.

How ironic that the World Cup of 1966 should do so much to inspire my ambitions to make it as a professional football only for the very same competition 16 years later to act as a catalyst for the ending of my playing career. I still love football even today, but from the moment I read that teletext announcement I never quite held the game in the same innocent affection. Football is a bruising business, but nothing else I endured during my playing career ever hurt anything like as much as what Billy Bingham did to me.

I have met Bingham in person just once since 1982. Thankfully, we were amongst a group of people so despite my loathing of the man I shook his hand and even ignored some clumsy comment he made about me once being "one of his boys".

My omission from the 1982 World Cup finals was the worst body blow I ever experienced in football and to aggravate the situation I was left with some tough decisions as to where I wanted to play my football and even whether I wanted to play football for a living any longer.

I felt lost, desolate even, and couldn't be consoled. I brooded about what I wanted to do with my life and informed Southend that I wanted to leave. If the manager was going to ignore me, I was not going to hang around to be humiliated.

Even though there was more football to be played in my career, my omission from the World Cup squad was the biggest snub I ever received, and I was never the same footballer again. The shabby treatment meted out to me by Billy Bingham left me feeling embittered. Never again would I take the same delight in the game.

Although Billy Bingham apologised in the Belfast Telegraph in the December of 1982 for the fact that he had not brought "whole-hearted players like Derek Spence or Eric MacManus" to the World Cup finals, his words were cold comfort for two good professionals coming to the end of their careers. The bare facts of the matter state that Bingham is the most successful Northern Ireland manager ever, but I very much doubt that he is the one who receives the greatest number of Christmas cards. I guarantee he will never get one from me.

Despite playing in the lower divisions throughout my career, I won 29 caps for my country, scoring three goals against Holland, Denmark and Wales respectively. I made appearances against countries as diverse as communist Yugoslavia, Israel, the great Dutch team of the seventies, and Australia. I featured several times against the home nations and in the first ever clash with the Republic of Ireland.

I played against the legendary Johan Cruyff and alongside the player I consider to be the best of all time, George Best. I was a long-term team-mate of some of the most distinguished Northern Ireland internationals in history, revered players such as Pat Jennings, Jimmy Nicholl, Sammy McIlroy and Martin O'Neill. I was managed by my childhood hero, Danny Blanchflower, travelled to countries I never dreamed of visiting, and made many lifelong friendships.

Nowadays, now that the pain has eased slightly, I look back with pride on my international career, but I will never forgive the man who denied me what should have been the pinnacle of my professional life. Less than three years later I was out of the game altogether.

My time at Southend was now over. In the main I loved it and I had a fantastic relationship with the supporters. My final goals in a Shrimper's shirt had been a brace versus Huddersfield Town in a 4-0 victory, but at the end of the 1981/82 season I was in a desperate place and even considering giving up football completely.

But out of the blue, I got a phone call from Robin Park, an Irish lad who was working as a journalist in Hong Kong of all places. He had contacts in a team called Hong Kong Rangers. They were looking for a new striker and Robin had been asked to approach me on their behalf. My attitude has always been one of, "Nothing ventured, nothing gained", so I decided to go and see what the Orient had to offer. Quite a few adventures as it turned out.

Chapter 13 [1982-1983]
Oriental adventures - Hong Kong Rangers

If Southend United didn't want me, Hong Kong Rangers certainly did. I was offered a contract from 1 August 1982 until 31 July 1983 on basic wages of £2,000 per month and a modest signing on fee. I duly agreed to go out and play a year for them. I knew that no matter what had happened in the last few months, I could still score goals and they needed a goal-scorer.

The team was made up of local Chinese lads and a mixture of mainly Scottish and Irish ex-pats. There was Jimmy Bone, who was an ex-Scottish international, and Brian Sinclair, who had been at Blackpool, so there was always going to be somebody around who spoke my language.

I joined up with my new teammates at their pre-season training in Sri Lanka of all places. We were based in Colombo, which was miles away from any of those palm-fringed, white sand beaches you might see in the travel brochures. In fact, it was a right dump. We did manage to get a day on the beaches and that was great, but most of the time we were based in dormitory style accommodation in some sort of guest house.

The Chinese lads seemed to be accustomed to sleeping six or eight to a room, but it was a bit of a shock to the European contingent, who were more used to having a room to themselves, or maybe sharing with one other person.

There were geckoes and all sorts of other lizards all over the place, and I remember one night I got such a shock when I saw a gecko in the toilet that I leapt into the air and came down on the toilet and knackered it. I didn't realise it at the time, but I had completely buggered it up, and the full extent of the damage only became apparent when we came back to the room a few hours later to find it knee deep in water. As you can imagine, I was not exactly Mr Popular at that point in time.

We played plenty of pre-season friendlies during our time in Sri Lanka and what I remember most of all was that the locals were not exactly the biggest lads I had played against. They were fit though; you had to give them that. Naturally, when you get two (or maybe that should be three) very different cultures coming together, things are going to get heated at some point.

And during one of these knockabout games, things got very heated indeed. One of the Chinese lads kicked one of the Sri Lankans in the head with a Kung Fu move that Bruce Lee would have been proud of. Naturally, the Sri Lankans, being on home turf and wanting to defend their honour, retaliated and before you could say, "Enter the Dragon", it kicked-off big style.

At that time there were just two Europeans on the pitch: yours truly with my white-blond hair and my mate John Watson, who just happened to have the reddest hair you have ever seen. We stood out like two Belisha beacons in a seething, writhing mass of black-haired people all hell bent on kicking the fuck out of each other. Eventually, when enough blood had been shed to assuage the affront, the hostilities abated and we were able to get on with the game again.

Sometime after that we were taken on a trip into the heart of the Sri Lankan rainforest. We were given a bit of a guided tour, the highlight of which was a ride on an elephant, complete with mahout and everything. However, my overriding memory was of the utter poverty. There were rats everywhere you looked. We always tried to give them a wide berth, but you could not avoid seeing them. Beggars lined the roads everywhere you went; some of them with quite horrific disabilities. It was clear to us that the only chance they had of earning a few coins was by going out onto the streets and begging.

I remember being quite afraid of these beggars for some reason and we used to walk down the middle of the road to avoid the roadside where they would all congregate. I realise now that I had absolutely nothing to fear from them but at that time I was not too far removed from the unsophisticated lad who had made his way out of Belfast a few years earlier.

Our accommodation in this rainforest resort was a vaguely westernised guest house. As you might expect, there was no entertainment, so if we wanted a night out or a bit of music, we used to go to a Holiday Inn-type place which was just down the road from our digs.

It was in Sri Lanka that I had my first encounter with chilli peppers. Back then I was still very much a meat and two veg man and the British high street had not yet become the multi-cultural food bazaar that it is today. Some of the Chinese lads took us for a meal. Naturally, they had grown up with chilli peppers as a part of their cuisine so when some of the Hong Kong based lads suggested that I try some, I grabbed a handful and started munching away.

Brian Sinclair did much the same thing. Nothing happened at first. Then I developed a tingling in my lips; next I started sweating and my face turned bright red. In a few moments I was struggling to breathe as my throat swelled in reaction to the burning acid of the chillies. For a minute I actually thought I was going to have a heart attack. There was no way any of my Chinese teammates could have warned me, as none of them spoke English. The club was too skint to supply an interpreter and there was no way I was ever going to be able to learn Chinese.

I don't know if it was as a result of the chilli episode, but eventually the club managed to stump up the cash for an interpreter, who then shadowed us wherever we went.

I got on really well with my Chinese colleagues once a means of communication had been established. I thought they were lovely blokes. Some of my European colleagues, however, would often take advantage - in our practice games - of their greater physical stature and kick lumps off their Asian counterparts. The worst culprit in all this was Jimmy Bone and he and I clashed a couple of times over his bully boy tactics.

Hong Kong Rangers were doing well in their own local league and the standard of football was really quite high. One of the other high-profile teams at that time was Seiko Sports Association, sponsored by the watchmakers of the same name. They had a few international players from Holland, Australia and the UK.

One of my more interesting experiences whilst I was out in the Far East was going to Singapore to play in an event called the Ho Ho Cup. This was a round robin tournament for teams that played their football in Hong Kong, Malaysia and Singapore. It was sponsored by the Ho Ho biscuit company.

For the duration of this tournament I shared a room with Brian Sinclair, the former Blackpool player. For some reason, none of the lads were keen to share a room with Brian. I soon found out why. Much as I liked him, there could be no denying that Brian had the smelliest feet in the world. The stench was awful. Although I went berserk when I found out why I had been made to share a room with him, in the end there was nothing I could do about it, no matter how much I ranted and raved.

In the end it worked out quite well. I nagged him to use deodorant and to be careful in his foot care routine, and with a combination of my instructions and proper ventilation, things became just about bearable.

When we arrived in Singapore for the tournament, one of the first things we did was to take a rickshaw ride around the city. During the trip our driver asked us if we would like to see "the cucumber show." Always game for a laugh, Brian and I agreed to see this local spectacle. It turned out to have nothing whatsoever to do with horticulture and a whole lot to do with culture of an altogether baser nature.

By this time, Brian and I were firm friends, what with having shared some of Singapore's rich cultural heritage. We even went out on the town for a drink on the eve of the big match: the Ho Ho Cup Final. Breaking curfew like that was something I had never done before, but since missing out on the World Cup, I was somewhat disillusioned with the game and was not quite the player I had once been in terms of attitude and application.

For the big match itself, I was due to start the game with Brian taking his place on the subs' bench. We were 1-0 down when I got injured in the first half as the result of a bad tackle, and Brian duly came on in my place. He made quite a favourable impression, scoring two spectacular goals that won us the game.

There was a big celebration after the game, but I could not help but notice that there was a bit of an atmosphere brewing with some of the Scottish lads. Naturally, where there is alcohol and bad feeling something is going to have to give. Suddenly there were tables, drinks and punches flying everywhere as it kicked off between the two warring factions. I can't imagine that the club's owners were very happy with the image we projected of their club and after that, when we went back to Hong Kong, there was always a bit of residual hostility left over from that night.

There were not too many serious games in the Hong Kong league. We seemed to play quite a lot of friendly games but even so, the regime was pretty strict and players had to toe the line with regard to training and the like.

Frances and the kids had come out to join me and, as I was the only one of our team who was married, things were a bit better for me, although I was a little unfair to Frances in all too often leaving her alone whilst I went out on the town.

We had our own little flat, and when I bought a Volkswagen beetle from a fellow ex-pat, I became the only European player with access to a car. I bought the beetle off a bloke who was a big cheese in the old Jardine Matheson Trading Company. This bloke was a Scot who lived right at the top of the Peak. Even I knew that the higher up the Peak you lived, the more important you were in Hong Kong society, so this fella must have been somebody special.

The car had belonged to his wife, who must have been ready for an upgrade to something more in keeping with her status. I paid about £1,000 for the car and was well pleased with my little runabout. It even had air conditioning.

When I went up to the top of the Peak to collect the car it was like something out of a James Bond film. As I approached the mansion, gates opened automatically and at the same time another car came out. The car belonged to the governor of Hong Kong, which only added to my sense of trepidation, but in the end we concluded the deal over a cup of tea, just like back home. Inevitably, the conversation got around to football and in particular the rumour that George Best would be returning to the island to ply his trade.

Bestie had played a game or two out in Hong Kong and had done very well. He was already deep into his well-documented battle with the booze, although at that time he was abstinent. I think he might have had some sort of implant in his stomach that would have made him violently ill in the event that he drank alcohol. I remember we had a couple of nights out and he stuck to drinking tea.

There had long been rumours that he was going to do a stint with us at Hong Kong Rangers and eventually those rumours turned out to be true.

George joined us for a month in the run in to the Hong Kong cup final. Naturally, being one of the most famous footballers ever to have laced on boots, brought with it some privileges. For example, he never had to attend morning training sessions. The rest of us were expected to be there at eight o'clock sharp, but Bestie was only required to be present at our regular evening training sessions.

The evening training sessions were conducted at Shah Tin, which was off Hong Kong Island. You had to get there via a tunnel and my little beetle came in handy as I ferried my team-mates to and from training. The traffic was horrendous and if you got caught in a jam during the rush hour you knew you were going to be stuck for a good while. The parking was also pretty problematic, with permits required for on-street parking. Once again, I was lucky as our little apartment had its own private car park.

Although Bestie did not have to attend morning training, that is not to say that he wasn't busy. He was busy all right: entertaining a non-stop stream of women who found their way to his hotel room day and night. It used to take two of us to get him out of there. His agent, Bill MacMurdo, would first ring his room and upon getting no reply he would go up to his room and hammer on the door. Meanwhile, I would station myself outside his window and shout up from the street below. Although he played hard to get, we knew he was in his room and I could hear his phone ringing as his agent tried to lure him out.

His preparation might have been unorthodox, but nobody could deny the effect he had on the team. When he did turn up for evening training, everybody had their spirits lifted by his mere presence.

Ever since being a little kid I have loved taking photographs and Bestie being with us for a month gave me the perfect excuse to upgrade my little camera for a better model and get some shots of my team-mates and the footballing deity who was to be briefly part of the team.

I bought an all-singing, all-dancing Nikon. The only trouble was, not only did I not know how to use it, I couldn't even put the film in. Naturally, when I bought it, the bloke in the shop put the first lot of film in for me. I took a few pictures of nothing in particular to get used to the thing and took the camera back to the same shop to get them developed.

However, now that the bloke in the camera shop took me for an experienced user, he assumed that I could put my own film in the camera. I was a grown man after all.

There I was taking all these souvenir photos of George Best, with me and my wife and two young children. I was going to put them in an album and maybe hand it down to my kids one day, so you can imagine my frustration then, when I took the camera back to the shop to get these precious snapshots developed, only to find that there had been no bloody film in the camera!

I have never sworn so fucking much in my life. I called the poor bloke in the shop all the names under the sun. I doubt he understood, but he must have got the gist.

Of course, it was my fault for assuming that the bloke had loaded the camera with film, as had been the case when I first bought it. Perhaps I was becoming a typical footballer: never thinking and always assuming that there would be somebody else on hand to accomplish even the simplest of tasks for me.

Later, I managed to see the funny side of my taking pictures of a footballing legend without any bloody film in the camera, but it took a few years to reach that state of grace. Thank fuck for digital cameras, I say.

We were playing well at that time and managed to get into the semi-final of the Hong Kong Cup, partly because we still had George Best playing for us on a game-by-game basis. This match was due to be played on a Sunday against local rivals, Seiko Sports Association.

The night before the big match we met up for a team talk at our training base in Shah Tin. Bestie was in the line-up for the semi-final and was expected to make a dramatic impact upon the game, so when the manager came out with the words, "… and that is when we take Best off...", you can imagine the consternation it caused. One of the local Chinese players would be replacing George at half-time, which, with the best will in the world, could hardly be regarded as a like-for-like swap. It seemed that the owners wanted to get their revenge on him for his unorthodox approach to training and other tedious duties.

I thought it unlikely that I was going to be sharing a pitch with Bestie ever again so, with the permission of the owners, I arranged for us to swap shirts after the match had finished. A shirt would make a much more tangible souvenir than a photo taken with a camera with no film in it. This was a bit before the days when shirt-swapping became established as a normal, post-match ritual.

George met us at the ground an hour before kick-off but was still unaware of plans to bring him off at half-time. It fell to me to give him the bad news that there was no way he was going to see out the whole game. He was absolutely livid.

Sure enough, at the end of the first-half with the score nil-nil, the management substituted the one and only George Best. They wanted to send a message that they could do whatever they pleased with their own players: no matter what they were called. I am sure that with the team at full strength, we could have won the game. As it was, Seiko ran out 1 - 0 winners.

Another set of owners had done the same thing at another club, taking off former England captain and World Cup winner Alan Ball, simply to show that they could do as they pleased with their assets.

For the handful of games he played for us, Bestie got a cheque for £15,000. He realised, however, that if he flew home with a cheque and there was some problem with it, sorting it out would be a very costly procedure. Bill MacMurdo demanded a banker's draft from the owners and, as they would have lost face if they had not agreed to pay it, he got what he wanted for his client. I agreed to drive George to the airport the following day in my trusty little beetle. The flight was due to leave at nine pm and, true to form, Bestie had to be dragged from his room an hour before take-off, leaving behind yet another groupie who would no doubt regale her friends with stories of a night of passion with a living footballing legend.

I have nothing but the fondest of memories of George Best. He was a lovely bloke. He was modest and charming and did not have the inflated ego of today's superstars. He was always on the side of the little fella. I remember one night when we were in a piano bar and the pianist had some sort of mild physical disability, a load of yobs were giving this bloke a hard time and taking the mickey in quite a nasty way. George went over and told them to knock it off in no uncertain terms. I was in regular contact with him by phone, right up until the time of his sad and premature death in 2005.

As things wound down for the end of the season in Hong Kong, it was time to take stock of where I was. I had to make a decision about whether to stay on for another year. I had got on well with my Chinese colleagues. They were a friendly bunch of lads and I certainly hope that they thought highly of me.

However, some of the training facilities were not up to much, and the local habit of making footballers do boxing-style roadwork on the hard, local surfaces of the hills leading up to the Peak had played havoc with my knees.

My wife and kids had had enough and with summer coming up fast, with all its heat and humidity, it was clearly time for a re-think. So, with the season not yet finished, I asked for permission to go home for a short while. Initially, this was just supposed to be to accompany my wife and kids on their return journey back to the UK, and in order to show my good intentions towards the club I agreed to use my trip to scout out a new winger, something they desperately needed.

Back in the UK with my wife and kids newly re-established in our house in Hambleton, I set about using my network of contacts in the lower leagues to find a suitable winger for Hong Kong Rangers. In the end I settled on a lad called Winston White. After a short break at home, I flew back to Hong Kong with Winston in tow. And that was when I got my first real experience of racism in football.

Shortly after my return, I got a call from one of the club's owners, a man by the name of Peter Chung. Apparently, some of the European players were not happy that Mr White was black. Not only that, but they were not too keen on having to share accommodation with him at the large apartment the club owned at Shah Tin. So, given that I still had a family apartment, but now no longer had a family with which to fill it, Winston moved in with me. It was the obvious solution and for the last three months of my contract Winston and I shared the club's big family flat.

In June my contract was up and even though it had been a good deal for me from a financial point of view, I didn't fancy a second year. After a bit of negotiation, the club paid me for June and July, which made it easier for them to sign a replacement.

I left Hong Kong and Winston White took over my old apartment. I think his girlfriend eventually came out to be with him, but then things started to go wrong. For some reason, which I could only conclude was based on the colour of his skin, the club refused to pay Winston what they owed him. So, being a resourceful sort of fella, Winston took it upon himself to recoup the money he was owed in the best way he could: he sold every movable item in the club flat! I was back in the UK at the time, so his actions had very little bearing upon me.

However, for financial reasons, I had to leave Britain for a while in order to avoid paying taxes on my Hong Kong earnings. I went back to Hong Kong, where I got a right bollocking from the club's owners about Winston's inventive way of making sure he got paid. They said Winston White was a very bad man. He wasn't at all. Their attitude towards him was disgraceful and he only did what any of us would have done to protect our interests.

If Winston's shabby treatment was all down to the colour of his skin, then more power to his elbow. I don't know what it must have been like for black players in the 70's and 80's and perhaps my earlier comment about my not having experienced racism was simply as a result of my not being able to see things from the perspective of those early pioneers. Despite the early exploits of high-profile black players like Cyrille Regis and Viv Anderson, football in Britain was still a profession dominated by white players. And as for the appointment of black managers - well let's just say that we still, even to this day, have some catching up to do in that regard.

I like to think of myself as a tolerant person. I certainly have no time for racism in any form and Hong Kong opened my eyes more than any other experience as to what it must be like to be on the receiving end of pure racism.

Chapter 14 [1983-1984]
Back to Bury - The twilight days

After my oriental adventure, it was back to my house in Hambleton with the wife and family around me and wondering what else was going to come my way. Leanna was now five and ready to attend school whilst Matthew was still a baby, so I needed to work and was hoping for some decent offers.

The last thing I was expecting was a phone call from the manager of Bury, Jim Iley. He must have heard that I was available I thought profoundly!

It had been a few years since my first proper grounding in professional football with the Shakers, but there were still a few familiar faces about the place.

Bury were having a very hard time of things on the pitch. They were in the old third division and if they were willing to take a punt on me, I was certainly happy to help my old club. They offered me a two-year contract from 25 August 1983 to 30 June 1985. The money was not that good, but I thought that the deal made sense on so many levels. There were also a few extras thrown in, such as a loyalty bonus and, all things considered, I was reasonably happy.

There were one or two high profile players with Bury at this time. They had signed Frank Carrodus from Man City and Terry Pashley, whom I already knew from Blackpool where he had been voted Player of The Year for three successive seasons.

Jim Iley was a genuine character. You never knew what he was going to say next. Pash proved to be an outstanding player for Bury, but on one memorable occasion, Jim, without warning, suddenly said to Terry "I don't really know why I signed you" before walking off without further comment.

Terry and I remain good pals to this day. In-fact he taught me to play tennis which I still enjoy. I continue in my refusal to play golf though because, frankly, I'm shite at the game. Indeed, during my life I have purchased six sets of golf clubs and sold them all. Well, you can't be good at everything can you?

And guess who else Bury signed? None other than my old mate Winston White!

I started off as a regular first teamer and, as was invariably the case, I managed to pick up an injury in the early part of the season. It was only a little knock to the ankle, but it tormented me.

Up until that time we had been doing quite well, especially in one cup game, when we managed a 0-0 draw at home to first division West Ham.

At this time, they had Frank Lampard senior, Billy Bonds and Trevor Brooking playing for them, so the home draw set us up nicely for the replay at Upton Park. Our goalie at the time was a lad called Dave Brown (I believe he now lives in Italy with his Italian wife). Dave was a lovely fella, but, unfortunately for us, he had broken a finger in a game immediately prior to the re-match. As we had no other reserve goalie available to us at the time, we were forced to take to the pitch with a goalie who was in agony every time a ball went anywhere near his hand.

Ten minutes after kick-off we were 4-0 down. They only had to cross a ball for it to go in. I remember that Tony Cottee had a field day, scoring four goals.

Luckily, we managed to go in at half-time only 5-0 down. Now, I don't know what a manager is supposed to say to his team in those circumstances to lift their spirits but the trouble was that Jim Isley didn't know either. I can't remember what he said, but whatever it was, it didn't bloody well work. We ended up on the wrong end of a 10-0 stuffing. At least it was a very even game: West Ham getting five goals in each half.

In addition to Cottee's handsome haul, Trevor Brooking and Alan Devonshire notched a brace apiece with Alvin Martin and Ray Stewart completing the scoring in my heaviest ever defeat. Indeed, I don't think I even lost a junior match by that margin.

Perhaps the best thing about it was the match report in our local paper: The Bury Times. According to them I was the pick of the forwards. I think they might have watched a different game. I don't know what I did to deserve such an accolade as I don't think I ever got in their half.

From that point onwards, I really struggled with form, injuries and, frankly, motivation.

We used to do a bit of road running as a part of our training and whereas in the old days I would usually have expected to be first across the line in such trials, by the time of my second spell at Bury I was coming dead last.

I realised that the writing was on the wall.

The precise nature of my ankle problem was never satisfactorily diagnosed. The lack of proper medical backup, something that had dogged me throughout my career, had reared its ugly head again.

Eventually, I decided to get the ankle looked at by a private consultant. He spotted a piece of bone floating around inside my ankle and told me that I would have to have an operation to remove it. I was completely disillusioned with football and with Bury for not giving me adequate medical support.

Naturally, I went to see Freddie Griffiths, who had helped me on so many previous occasions. I was just 32 years old, but with the help of Freddie, I decided it was time to get out of football. The ankle injury merely provided the hook upon which to hang the decision. If I went out of the game with an injury retirement, there was just a chance that I might be able to get some compensation. Bury might even be able to get some compensation for losing my services.

As it turned out, Bury didn't even have me insured which grated plenty. As luck would have it, though, the Professional Footballers' Association was able to help. They offered me a lump sum pay out of ... £1,500!

Thankfully, there was also a regular pension payment of something like £8 per week to soften the blow. Clearly, I was not going to enjoy a celebrity retirement.

I took the lump sum from the PFA and Bury managed to pay me for the time left to run on my contract and that was that. I was now an ex-footballer.

With the benefit of hindsight, I later realised that getting out of football was just about the worst mistake I ever made. I had the operation, and with a decent rest over the summer the ankle healed and was fine again. I even played a bit of amateur football with Oldham Town in the North West

Counties League as if to tell myself that I was still capable of playing the game I had always loved.

Alternatively, I should have gone into coaching, but memories of the way I had been treated by Billy Bingham were still too fresh in my mind. If being a coach or a manager meant treating people like dirt, it was clearly not for me.

Whilst finalising this book the financial troubles that Bury had been facing came to the fore and ending with their expulsion from the Football League. As for all Shakers fans this news was deeply upsetting for me, and I sincerely hope that a way can be found to re-establish the club to resurrect it once more as a playing force worthy of its proud history.

Chapter 15 [1984-1987]

What next? - Living without football

So, being the archetypal business wizard, I did what every former international footballer does: I bought a corner shop in Bury.

My little shop was on Walmsley Road, Bury, and amongst other things it provided me with an excellent opportunity to find out just how little I knew about life outside football and, in particular, about the retail trade. I asked my sister, Joan, and her husband to come over from the Isle of Man to help me run it. They agreed to do this, and together we all found out just how much we had to learn.

The first problem was the nature of the property itself. It was a great big old place, which was going to take some maintenance. And my sense of timing was not great. This was the time that saw the rise of the supermarkets to their current position of total dominance in the retail world. The only way you could possibly make any money out of a shop like this was to keep it open all hours. So, just like Ronnie Barker's `Arkwright', that is what I did.

I had invested pretty much all of the money I had taken out of football and I soon found that living 40-odd miles away in Hambleton and working all the hours in a day was not a recipe for success. We had three lots of wages going out of the business. And the local scallies, who imagined that I was some multi-millionaire, played their part by robbing me blind. I was a sitting duck.

Thankfully, I managed to buy a couple of old houses and with a mate called Keith Bell, who was a brickie, I was able to do them up and sell them. That was the only bright spot on the horizon.

Naturally, I employed the best accountants and solicitors to look after my interests. They too, must have thought I had been on the same sort of wages that Lionel Messi gets today and, rather than look after my interests, they looked after their own and charged me some exorbitant rates.

But I wasn't going to be put off by these setbacks and I certainly wasn't afraid of hard work. I really did work some long hours and, in addition, even managed to remodel the interior of the shop to make it more suited to its purpose.

As a retailer my crafty trick was to pay too much money for my stock and I compounded my woes by selling that stock too cheaply. I think I must have got some old retailing advice the wrong way around. Bills were coming in from the accountant every month and, pretty soon, we were haemorrhaging money.

My brother Alex had witnessed an IRA shooting at a football match and was badly affected by the trauma of the incident. The poor lad had to have a lot of counselling and eventually, thanks partly to Daddy pleading with me to take him over the water to begin a new life, he came over to England and briefly lived with me in Bury.

Initially, Alex tried to make it as a pro footballer, but although he was scouted by both Manchester United and Liverpool he never made the grade. He was always keen to run forward but lacked any enthusiasm for working back to fulfil his defensive duties, so despite the famed scout Bob Bishop describing him as the next Liam Brady he disappeared from the game forever.

I found Alex some work in my Bury off-licence and he also did some labouring. We remain close, as Alex only lives about 30 minutes away so we manage to meet up regularly.

At around this time I went through something that was to change my life for the worse: I was convicted of assault. Naturally, I am not proud of this incident, but if I tell the truth about what happened, I will leave it to the reader to decide if they think I am a bad person.

I had just finished my footballing career at Bury and was in the process of trying to get rid of the off license. I was burning the candle at both ends and the only chance I got to relax was at the end of the evening when, along with a friend of mine called Bob, who owned a fish and chip shop, I would go out for a couple of pints.

We would drive to Somerset Liberal Club in an old banger that Bob used to have. Naturally, when I say a couple of pints, what I meant was seven or eight. I don't know where Bob put it, as he was only a skinny bloke, but I could never keep up with him and his prodigious thirst.

At the time of the incident we had been going to the club for about a year and most of our time there was spent playing pool and generally chewing the fat.

For some reason, on this particular night we were playing snooker which was not our game at all. Three lads walked in and challenged us to a game of snooker: a challenge we readily accepted. These lads could really play a bit and they hammered us with ease. Then the abuse started: "Did people really pay money to see you play?" And from that it progressed to, "Irish bastard, why don't you fuck off back to Ireland?"

Wanting to avoid confrontation, I replied: "Alright, lads, you have had your fun, but that is the end of it." I thought that it might have ended there, but as I went to the toilet one of these lads said something particularly offensive. I just reacted without thinking and lashed out. Unfortunately for both of us, I had my snooker cue case in my hand and even more unfortunately, it had my snooker cue in it. The blow landed full force and split the lad's head wide open.

Now I have always relished the physical side of the game of football and I always knew how to look after myself on the pitch. I have had the odd fight off the pitch as well, but I had, until that time, always used my fists alone. This was a moment of madness. Somebody pushed me a little bit too far on a night when I was tired and stressed out about getting rid of the off license. This was not a premeditated thing.

The lad's mates all legged it at the first sign of any trouble and the lad himself must have called the police. I was arrested at about two o'clock in the morning and taken from my house to the police station in Bury, where I was fingerprinted. It was pretty embarrassing, all the coppers knew me but there was nothing I could do about that.

When it went to court, my solicitor told me to plead guilty. He reckoned I had to own up. But as these lads were well known to the police, my brief thought that would count as mitigating circumstances and I would get off lightly, with a small fine or something similar. With hindsight, I should have pleaded not guilty and maybe got a better solicitor who could have made a case for self-defence. I had, after all, been subjected to some pretty extreme provocation. But as a young man with a business to run and a family to look after, I took the easy option.

I bitterly regret that decision now, as that incident still shows up on my DBS forms all these years later. In the end I was fined £100 and was ordered to pay costs. Of course, the press had a field day and the local paper ran the headline: "Footballer guilty of assault!" It even made the papers out in Hong Kong. I was devastated and ashamed.

Despite the odd provocation that naturally ensues when wannabe tough guys spot a current or ex footballer on a night out, I have thankfully had very few scrapes with the Neanderthals in our midst. I remember during my time at Blackpool sometimes coming out of the Tangerine Club and, following a home loss that day no doubt, running the gauntlet as a few pissed-up and pissed-off fans shouted some abusive criticism in my direction. That led to a few brief skirmishes but the majority of times, after a colourful exchange of views, things simmered down and peace prevailed.

I've never looked for trouble and, despite my temper, bar the odd scrap here and there, I've invariably kept my cool and stayed out of trouble. Which made the court case all the more upsetting, particularly as I felt I was the injured party.

Over the years I've mellowed a lot and now believe that I'm Mr Average in the Mr Angry stakes.

Anyhow, with one thing and another, we were soon left with no alternative but to sell my lovely house in Hambleton and move into the accommodation above the shop. I bought my sister a little terraced house just down the road and her husband managed to find some work, and these new circumstances gave us a bit of breathing space.

This situation went on for two years. Eventually, I managed to make a good job of improving the upstairs accommodation and completely restructuring the shop itself.

In the middle of all this, I got a surprise call from the owners of Hong Kong Rangers, who wanted me to go back out and play for them on a game-by-game basis. The pay would have been somewhere in the region of £800 a week if I stayed injury free, but I had made my decision to retire and, regretfully, I told them I would not be taking them up on their offer. Just after that phone call I had a reminder that life was not all about money. At the back of Bob's chippy there was a manhole cover that gave access to the general sewage system and Bob must have been having a bit of trouble with his drains because he had a plumber round to do some work on it.

Somehow or other the water level had risen-up until it was overflowing from the manhole cover. The plumber took the cover off in order to access the blockage and then, for some reason, was called away. My son, Matthew, who was about three years old at the time, was playing with Bob's son at the back of the chippy. Matthew never realised the depth of the water, and for some reason he decided to investigate. The next thing anybody knew he had fallen in and was in the filthy water up to his eyeballs, screaming and crying his eyes out. Bob's son was nowhere to be seen.

Somehow or other, Matthew managed to get a grip on something and haul himself out onto dry land, where he stood dripping and shivering and soaked from head to toe in freezing cold water. Given the depth of the water in the drain at the time, it could have been so much worse. I don't go to church very much these days, but that afternoon I found time to go and take a pew and offer up a silent prayer of thanks to the man upstairs.

After three years of running the shop I decided to sell up. I had managed to get the takings up and the building itself was now looking very nice. Property prices had been going up for a while, so it was a good time to sell. It looked like I could at least break even on the deal.

I had some prospective buyers lined up and for some reason they had elected come around on a Sunday. When the day of the viewing dawned it was raining. It continued to rain without let-up for three or four hours. Somehow the rain started to leak into the roof and from there down through to the ceiling, which started to drip ominously. Suddenly, there was water everywhere as the ceiling gave way under the weight of water. I got a mop and bucket and cleaned up the mess as best as I could, but it was hardly a good impression to give to our prospective buyers.

For whatever reason, the viewers decided that they weren't bothered about the flood and they ended up buying the shop in a part exchange deal. As part of the deal, we moved into their old house in the Walmsley area of Bury, which was the nice end of town.

By this time, I was rapidly approaching 40 and was still not really sure what I wanted to do with my life. At the time I had no mortgage, but neither did I have any income. I had learnt a few things about buying and selling and my experience with solicitors and accountants had taught me just how expensive the services of those professionals could be.

Whilst I was pondering my future and generally engaging in a bit of navel gazing, I got a phone call from a bloke called Sam Salt. Sam had played football for Blackpool in the '60's but I knew him from living in Hambleton, where he had an off license. It turned out that Sam had another shop that he wanted me to buy. The difference this time around was that I knew what I was letting myself in for. The shop in question was in Hambleton, where I had lived previously.

The turnover was £200,000 per year and, even more attractively from my point of view, the opening hours were much shorter: from twelve till two at lunch time and then an evening session from six till ten. It sounded like a doddle compared to the other place. I ended up buying the freehold and also had to pay £60,000 for the goodwill alone, which was quite a lot to pay in 1987.

I hoped that people would come in through the front door for a chat. Of course, it would be even better if they bought a few things while they were at it. In the end that was how it worked out. I was still quite well known in the area having played for Blackpool and people seemed to enjoy buying their beer and fags from a former footballer.

I had to put up with the occasional ignorant comment. This was particularly noticeable after any atrocity in England. On one occasion, after an IRA bombing hit the news, some idiots congregated outside the shop shouting, "I see your lot have been at it again!" By then, I had been living in England on and off for 17 years. I came from the unionist side of the Northern Ireland divide and was therefore as appalled as any Englishman by IRA outrages and to top it off, my mother was English! As a result, I remember being angry with the morons who made those comments, but on the whole, I was well received by the people of Hambleton and I like to think that I was popular with them.

As is so often the case, when things are going well, providence has a way of showing you not to get too complacent. My much-loved brother-in-law, Aubrey, was suddenly taken ill.

Chapter 16 [1987]
Deaths in the family and life gets harder

In December 1986 I got a phone call from my eldest sister, Isabella. She still lived in Belfast and was ringing to tell me that her husband, Aubrey, had been diagnosed as having lung cancer. Aubrey was quite well known in Belfast as the owner of O'Hara's Bakery: a chain of bakers with some 40 shops dotted around Belfast.

He had worked hard and managed to get a great standard of living for his family. He had a beautiful house and I remember he had just been on a trip to Germany to buy special light fittings for his home.

Aubrey and my sister had four young kids and this sad news devastated us all.

I went over to Belfast to see the family, knowing by this time that the writing was on the wall. I had never forgotten that Aubrey had bought me my first kit bag on the eve of my international debut for the Northern Ireland youth team many years ago, so perhaps it was for that reason that I took over one of my few remaining international caps (I had lost or given away most of them by then) and gave one to Aubrey and his family. On the same visit I also gave caps to my other brothers-in-law.

I sat and talked to Aubrey and we chatted about life in general. His only regret was, that as a result of his workload, he had never found the time to take his kids to Disneyland. Previously, I had advised Aubrey on a couple of occasions that he should take things a bit easier, failing completely to see the irony of the fact that, over the last few years, I too had been working seven days a week.

Aubrey was a lovely, lovely guy. I thought the world of him. He was a fantastic husband to Isabella, and he adored her and the kids. He would have done anything for them and worked hard to provide them with as good a life as possible.

Aubrey died on the 13th May 1987, just three months after his diagnosis. We were all devastated. He had never been a smoker, so that could be ruled out as a cause, but I am certain that a job he once did with my Daddy could well have been a factor.

Daddy and Aubrey did some demolition work in one of Aubrey's shops and some foul substance had come down out of the roof and left them both coughing up black phlegm for days afterwards. Aubrey, grafter that he was, had no need to get involved with the job, but he just could not see work being done without feeling the need to pitch in. That work ethic might have been the cause of his illness. My conviction, that whatever they had breathed in that day had been highly toxic, seemed to be borne out, when Daddy was also diagnosed with lung cancer a short while later.

Daddy was 67 when he received his prognosis. There had been something wrong with his chest for a while but, like so many men, he had ignored it and tried to battle through. His treatment was progressing very slowly in Belfast and I was desperate to try and do something, anything, to help.

I decided to take matters into my own hands. Who did I call? Why none other than Freddie Griffiths, of course. I owe so much to that man.

Freddie made a couple of phone calls and said if I could get Daddy over to Manchester the following day, a consultant at Wythenshawe hospital would take a look at him. I didn't need any second thoughts on the matter. Daddy was taken into hospital and they removed the cancerous lung there and then. The speed of this whole thing was purely as a result of Freddie's intervention. But, sadly, it was a case of too little, too late.

Daddy convalesced with us for a while in Hambleton and, when he felt well enough, he went back to Belfast. My sister, Doris had been living in Shaw, near Oldham, but had already decided to return to Belfast as she wanted her kids to be educated there, so it was Doris who accompanied Daddy back to Northern Ireland.

I remember we hired a big removals van to get all her stuff back to Belfast. I drove the van and was able to have one last conversation with Daddy. He gave me all his carpenter's tools, which I still have to this day. He knew he was no longer going to need them. I had to have the removals van back in England by the Monday morning and so we said our goodbyes and I never saw him again. He died on 2nd August 1988. The fact that I had to leave so abruptly still hurts to this day.

I loved my Daddy dearly. He never said too much about my achievements, but he was very proud of me, I know that. The best moments we shared - and the ones which made me realise just how much pride he took in my career - were when he turned up at games unexpectedly. He delighted in surprising me although it was him in shock when he turned up at one game (at Crewe I think when I was playing for Blackpool) and it had just been called off. He was a Liverpool fan but, unfortunately, I never played against them which was a blow because I'd have loved to have had him there watching me play against his team.

Daddy was real character. He loved arranging parties - causing Mum even more cooking as a consequence. I can still remember now, Daddy the life and soul of the assembly, Isabella singing whilst helping Mum cook yet more incredible food.

In a very short space of time two members of my family had died of lung cancer. I am sure that whatever fell out of that roof was a contributory factor, but I also think that neither of them was helped by their seven day a week workload. I remember having a conversation with Daddy one day and telling him that I thought he should take some time off. He said, "I tell you what, son, I'll give up Sunday mornings!"

Daddy had always loved his work, although I suspect that part of that was due to the fact that, if he was working, he could always pop into the pub on the way home and have a pint and a chinwag with his mates.

These events prompted me to have a good hard look at my own life. I too was working seven days a week and something was going to have to give. Did I want to work until I dropped? I didn't really think the question was too hard to answer so I sold the business to some local people for a good price and embarked on the start of yet another new era.

Chapter 17 [1988-1996]
What happens now? Jobs, I've had a few but not too few to mention

The big question was: what the hell to do next? In the end the answer was quite a long time coming.

I tried my hand at all sorts of things from labouring to taxi driving. I got involved in various unlikely and unworkable enterprises and I often wonder how many former international footballers end up working with their hands as a humble labourer.

An American bloke I knew called Jim Adams had just bought a franchise called Chem-dry, which was a carpet and upholstery cleaning business. He asked if I would like to do a bit of work with him on the franchise and, not having anything better to do with my time, I agreed.

One day, after I had been working with Jim for about two months, he said to me: "Derek, why are you always so happy in the mornings? You never seem to have any problems." I just told him that was the way I was. I just like to get on with life. Then he asked me another question, "What do you think of the Chem-dry business?" I told him I thought it was the most boring fucking thing I had ever done in my life. To my surprise, he agreed with me and when he asked me if I wanted to buy the business from him, I told him that I would rather stick my dick in a blender.

Jim was obviously finding the upholstery business pretty boring himself and it was clear that with the money he had to pay for the franchising rights, he wasn't making much profit on the venture either. Jim and I got on really well: he was a bit of a one-off. He could speak German and had all sorts of unusual interests. Six months later, he managed to sell the franchise to some poor bugger and went back to the USA. I never heard from him again.

A local lad called Mark Wrathall whose wife, Tracey, worked in the off-license, had just bought into a local taxi company called Blacktax. He was looking for a driver and as it was clear that cleaning carpets and upholstery was never going to work, I took the taxi drivers' test for Blackpool and the surrounding area. The test was a piece of cake and suddenly I was a cabbie.

Once again, I was offered the opportunity to buy into a business. There were just two things standing in my way.

The first difficulty was that I am stone deaf. I don't know if years of aggressively heading a football were to blame but whatever the reason my hearing was not up to the job. Even with one of those old-fashioned NHS hearing aids in each ear, I could not hear the dispatcher. The radio would squawk, "Red six, Box four" and I wouldn't hear it. And I would ask, "Did you say me, luv?" and the dispatcher would be going off her rocker.

The second drawback was my tendency to love a chat. I would pick up a fare and talk them to death. They couldn't get out of the bloody cab for me rabbiting on at them. We would get to the destination and I would still be rabbiting away. Sometimes the customers would invite me in for a cup of tea and that would be that. I was never going to make any money in a month of Sundays.

The driving side of things had never been the problem, so I decided to take my HGV license. I booked my lessons with a bloke who had his own lorry for the purposes of teaching the HGV course. I was lucky in that the PFA paid for all my lessons and they were generally a big help to me at that time, assisting me with all sorts of things and paying for courses and the like. The test itself is difficult and, in common with a lot of other people I took a couple of attempts to pass.

On the first occasion, I hit the kerb going into the test centre, which is an automatic fail. I always reckoned it was the fault of the silly bugger who had parked so close to the entrance of the centre.

On my second attempt the examiner was a much stricter bloke who asked me all sorts of complicated questions about the hydraulic systems on these big wagons. I had learnt, in parrot fashion, all the answers to the questions I was expecting so I didn't have a clue as to what he was on about when he asked questions I hadn't rehearsed answers to. I hadn't anticipated an examiner who would be so thorough in his questioning. I didn't even understand the questions and confessed as much to the examiner. I explained that I was doing the HGV test merely as a backup if other plans didn't work out. I only wanted to drive the lorries, not to take them apart.

I must have convinced him of my good intentions, because he passed me but not before warning me in no uncertain terms that if I ever did go out on the road I had better learn about the mechanics of these big wagons beforehand. It only occurred to me later that the test date had coincided with the anniversary of my Daddy's death: the second of August. Perhaps Daddy had been looking out for me from wherever he was billeted.

I thought it might be a good idea to get a bit of experience of driving big wagons and, as luck would have it, one of my old footballing mates, David Holt, who had been with me at Bury and performed the duties of best man at my wedding, now had a plastics factory in Haslingden and needed a driver. I went working for him for a while, but after a week or so, I realised that the responsibility of driving these massive lorries with loads of potentially highly dangerous substances was never going to be my cup of tea. I also don't like spending large parts of the day alone. I had always been used to being part of a team and I struggled to adapt to the enforced solitude. So that little venture went out of the window.

Once more I found myself at a loose end and asking myself what the bloody hell I was going to do with myself.

At that time the IRA had set off some bombs in Manchester city centre, which had done terrible damage. There was plenty of work to be had in rebuilding the Arndale Centre and one or two other places that had been either damaged or levelled in the blast. So, for a while, I was labouring, filling up skips in Manchester with Donald Anton, a schoolboy friend and lifetime mate. I quite enjoyed it. Don't forget that I had started out as a chippie.

Whilst I was labouring in Manchester, I decided to study for my coaching badges. I managed to get my UEFA "B" license But, typical of my confused plans for the future at that time, I had no ambitions to coach teams. I much preferred the prospect of getting the best out of youngsters on an individual basis. The team tactics stuff was never going to be my thing. The FA-way of doing things, with all the tactics written out beforehand and coaches advised not to act solely on their instincts, was an anathema to me. What I knew I would enjoy was coaching an individual with average ability and turning him or her into a half-decent player.

I went down to see a couple of old colleagues from Southend United and they showed me the ropes with regards to running soccer schools. Southend had had great success with these schools, and they were clearly on to something. After learning all I could down on the South coast, I came back home ready to give it a try.

I ran my first school at Bispham High School in Blackpool where the head teacher, Mrs Berry, was an enthusiastic proponent of all sporting activities. Bispham High was an all-girls school that had previously been known as Greenlands. I thought the co-educational school - Beacon Hill - just down the road may have made a better venue, but they didn't seem to be interested.

The immediate success of this venture provided me with the encouragement I needed to branch out further. In the end I worked in partnership with Bispham High for a total of 15 years.

At this time mini soccer was all the rage so I set up my own company - Derek Spence Sportslink - and opened my first mini soccer school in Fleetwood. This was one of the first such centres on the Fylde coast. Everybody said that I would only be able to manage one place on my own and nobody seemed to believe that I could manage more than one. Always ready for a challenge, I ended up with six centres. I soon found out just how big a workload that represented but I was enjoying life, mainly because I was my own boss and didn't have to take orders from anybody else.

1996 was a very eventful year for me. Things had not been going well between Frances and me for some time. This was possibly something to do with her asking me to have a vasectomy. Frances did not want any further children, but I did not necessarily want to put an end to that particular chapter of my life. I come from a big family and was always used to having a busy household. I love kids and the thought of having more held no terrors for me. Frances never got over the fact that I refused to have my plumbing tinkered with, and eventually we decided to split up.

At the time of the split, I had bought some derelict property in Fleetwood: four shops with accommodation above. The idea being that I would renovate them with a mate of mine who was a builder. As a result of my marital situation, I moved into one of the flats. I was 44 years old and a bachelor again.

I carried on paying Frances' mortgage for five years after we split up, on account of the fact that she refused to grant me a divorce until we had been apart for that duration. In the end we split things amicably on a 50-50 basis. She kept the house in Hambleton and I retained the flats in Fleetwood.

Much as I would have loved my kids to come and live with me, I thought that the fairest thing for them and their future was for them to live with their mum. I never ducked my financial responsibilities as far as the kids were concerned and our years of living apart don't seem to have damaged my relationship with them.

Given that Leanna is now a deputy head of a local school and Matthew also has a good job within the education system, I think that the decision to let the kids stay with their mum was the right one. I must give credit to Frances for being a fantastic mum and a stabilising influence on the children.

For my part, I was not a great husband to Frances. I was immature, too wrapped up in my career and, like most sportspeople, very selfish. At times, I went out too much leaving Frances on her own. This was particularly the case in Hong Kong.

We eventually grew apart but did share some great times. We holidayed in the South of France, on one occasion driving down (as you do) in a Triumph Spitfire, another in a Ford Capri towing a caravan, and we have two fabulous children as a legacy of our time together. I am genuinely delighted that Frances has since re-married and found happiness.

Living alone gave me plenty of time to think. Too much. All this navel-gazing did not suit me and I was soon drinking more than was good for me. Eventually, I realised that whatever the question was, the answer was not likely to be found at the bottom of a bottle.

My way out of this situation was to throw myself into work with renewed vigour. I can remember all this very clearly, because, unusually, we had very deep snow in Fleetwood that year. There was plenty of work to do in the little flat and I spent a fair amount of time redecorating and generally sprucing the place up. It is a long time ago now, but I can still remember that cold, lonely winter as if it was yesterday. But after winter comes spring and so it was with me.

Chapter 18 [1996]
Mauritius - One last footballing fling

Living alone in the cold did little for my mood, so when I got a phone call from Bryan Hamilton, the Northern Ireland manager at the time, I did not have to think too long about his proposal. Did I, he wondered, fancy an all-expenses paid trip to Mauritius?

I looked around at my surroundings and the decision was not too hard to make.

The invitation was to be part of an all-star, seven-a-side football competition held in Mauritius. The event was sponsored by Air Mauritius; a luxury holiday company by the name of Beachcomber Holidays and, as luck would have it, the island's most prestigious brewery, Phoenix. As it turned out, the workforce at the brewery probably got a fair bit of overtime out of our visit.

The invited teams were intended to represent; Manchester City, Manchester United, Spurs, a London All-Stars outfit, and a Northern Ireland team of which I was to be a part. This was probably the greatest display of footballing talent ever to visit Mauritius. Some of the stars on display were Willie Donachie, Asa Hartford, Viv Anderson, Joe Jordan, Phil Parkes, Martin Chivers and Eddie Gray. Plus Gerry Armstrong and me from Northern Ireland.

It was a seven-day trip and we played five or six teams, depending on how far into the tournament each team got. By this time I had been out of professional football for about

12 years. The rest of the lads were a mixture of retired and active footballers.

From day one the camaraderie and the craic were excellent. It was a laugh-a-minute experience and just what I needed. Apart from playing a few seven-a-side games of football, there were no further claims on our time. This distinctly non-punishing schedule meant we were free to make the most of the entertainments on offer. These included deep sea fishing, tennis, a golf tournament and even a spectacular night at the island's famous casino. The local brewery made sure that we were never more than a few inches away from a bottle of their finest lager, and when we went to the casino, we didn't even have to buy our own gambling chips.

The hotel we stayed in was one of those tropical island paradise jobs, all open-sided shacks with thatched roofs and palm trees. This was the first place I ever encountered an infinity pool. Some of the main accommodation blocks were modelled on the traditional houses of Mauritius. Large, cool airy spaces were patrolled by smartly uniformed staff, whose sole purpose was to attend to the guests' every whim. Those whims usually took the form of either cocktails or beers where our lads were concerned. It's fair to say that we were happy the whole time we were there.

The records for the trip showed that we drank a total of 7,500 bottles of beer in five days. This worked out at an average of over 20 bottles per day, per man. Given that some of the lads did not drink, you can see just how diligently those who did partake applied themselves to the task in hand. On many nights we stayed in the hotel bar until six in the morning.

One of the local skills we were keen to acquire was the skill of bartering with the trinket sellers who patrolled the beach from dawn till dusk. Most of what they sold was worthless tat - bronze ornaments and necklaces of sharks' teeth and the like. It turns out that the vendors were not greedy for money: what they wanted was to swap their merchandise for branded western goods. A pair of training shoes or a branded t-shirt could get you a mountain of souvenirs, so I was pretty chuffed to get rid of some old trainers in return for about a hundredweight of baubles, bangles and beads.

It was only when I got back to the bar that I realised that my bartering skills had let me down. I had forgotten that I usually leave my hearing aid in my shoes, to keep it from getting wet whilst on the beach, so some itinerant Mauritian trinket vendor not only had my old training shoes, but he also had my beige NHS hearing aid. The lads thought this was extremely funny and took the piss mercilessly for the rest of the trip.

The football was only meant to be semi-serious, but when you get professionals involved, even friendly games end up with a bit of an edge to them. Sometimes there were some very strong challenges flying in and the usual squaring up to the assailant and having to be separated by team-mates. But what do you expect when you are playing with the likes of Joe Jordan and Mick Harford?

I knew I had not calmed down completely after one game and the unofficial report of the tournament records that in the wee small hours of the morning I suggested to Mick Harford that we all go down to the beach and kick fuck out of one another. Legend has it that I was stark bollock naked at the time.

When the tournament was over and we were on our way to the airport, Bryan Hamilton surprised me by offering me a first class seat on the plane. The rest of the lads in tourist class had to pass me on the way to their seats and so you can imagine that the banter was pretty fierce.

I owe a big thank you to Bryan for offering me the chance to lift my spirits with this trip, which came at a time when I was feeling pretty down in the dumps. Looking back on it now, I think how special it was to have been involved with an event that brought together 57 top footballers. All of these players were ones who had come up through the various British youth teams. Not a single one of them was a signing from a foreign club. These days, if top teams sent a selection of their best players to a tournament, the big question would be, what percentage of them would be home-grown?

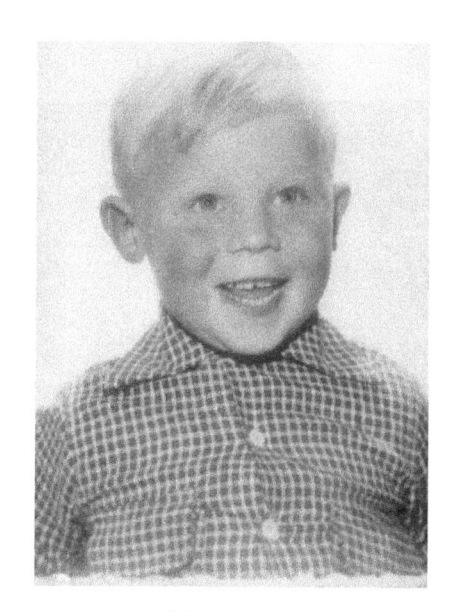

Me Aged 4

Me Aged 10

Irish youth team - leaving for Scotland

Oldham Athletic - first professional club

Bury promotion winning team 1973

Definitely the best goal of my career scored for Bury against Barnsley ..... some people say the best goal that has ever been scored at Gigg Lane.

My debut for Blackpool against Brian Clough's Nottingham Forest

Me with Paul Hart - Starsky and Hutch!!!

Off to Greece - Olympiakos

Back to Blackpool - Under Bob Stokoe

Northern Ireland squad 1979

Scoring a header for Blackpool

And another

Republic of Ireland v Northern Ireland in Dublin - with Mark Lawrenson

Same match - against Liam Brady

My team-mate in Hong Kong - absolute legend

Southend - Division 4 Champions Season 80/81

Me with the Division 4 winners trophy ... and a perm!!!!

Second spell at Bury and my last professional club

Northern Ireland vs England against Colin Todd

Me with my beloved Mummy and Daddy

My beautiful sisters … (from left to right) Joan, Isabella, Diane, Doris and Maureen

My little Brother Alexander (far left), with the main man.

Me and my beloved Alf

Lyn and I at Michaels wedding

My first born ... Leanna

My eldest lad Matthew

Starting again!! With Tom

Last but certainly not least … Erin

My Community work, at the regional finals of the Football League Kids Cup with Carters Charity Primary School

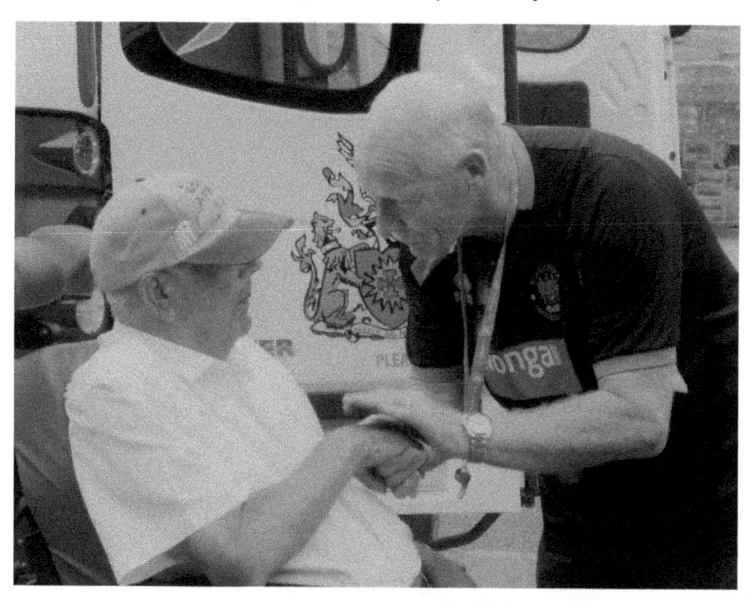

My NCS work for the Community Trust

Love my walking football

My after-dinner antics

Still playing at 67!!!

Chapter 19 [1996]
Back to Bloomfield Road and other adventures - Enjoying life again

As I have already reflected, the year I relocated to Fleetwood and split up from my first wife, Frances, was an eventful one. And that was when a job came up at my old club, Blackpool.

The job title was Community Officer. The current incumbent, Craig Madden, was leaving and recommended that I apply for the job. When I applied for the position, Blackpool must have been very relieved, as at that time I was, in effect, the competition with regards to community coaching. My new role would be to get the local community involved in football, playing, coaching and watching.

Blackpool FC's Chief Executive Officer was a woman called Gill Bridges, and Vicky Oyston, wife of owner, Owen Oyston, was the chairperson. The interview turned out to be a case of me interviewing them and seeing how the job on offer suited my plans. They knew I had the edge over them with regards to running community-based skills and coaching programmes, so it was more of a question of 'Could we work together?'

Although I worked out of an office in Bloomfield Road, I was not employed by Blackpool FC. My official employer was 'Football in the Community' (FitC), an organisation based from the PFA offices in Manchester. This was a self-funding project: in other words, my salary depended entirely upon my bringing in the necessary income. The only money the project received was £6,000 per annum, to go towards the most basic expenses.

I had written a business plan and worked out all the figures and projections. The ambition previously had been to earn around £15,000 per annum from the scheme. I bravely told FitC that I would aim to bring in £50,000 a year! In the end I was bringing in £55,000 so my bravado was justified. And that was with no support staff.

Because of the surplus I generated, I was able to recruit another full-time member of staff. Her name was Lyn Forster. She had just finished her sports science course at college, but I had actually known her family from the time when I ran the off license in Hambleton and she had worked for me coaching tennis and multi-sports at my soccer schools at Bispham High. She took on the role of Assistant Community Officer.

It was around this time too that I bumped into my old pal and ex Blackpool team-mate, Wayne Harrison. I hadn't seen him for over 16 years, ever since I had gone to Southend, but when we unexpectedly met up again it was like we'd always been mates, we got on that well. Wayne was looking to break into coaching, so I offered him a job and and he soon became a massive asset.

Wayne is a brilliant lad and he and his wife have become great friends with Lyn and me. He later moved to the USA, where he still lives, but we have stayed in touch and Lyn and I have travelled to America to see him and his family on several occasions.

I even had the chance to start playing a bit of football again after a long layoff. A group of lads based on the Fylde Coast had a Sunday League football team called Fleetwood Car Centre, which was run by Steve Abbott and John Evans – the owners of the eponymous business.

This team had a number of ex professional footballers in its ranks, including players who had played in the highest echelons of the English football league. One such player was ex Crewe Alexandra centre half Steve Macauley. Having been rejected as a teenager by Manchester City, despite being part of the famous 1986 Youth Cup winning squad which comprised of players such as Paul Moulden, Paul Lake, Steve Redmond and Ian Brightwell, by Dario Gradi and played as high as Division Two (now the Championship).

Steve finally finished his playing career with a return to Fleetwood Town, the old Fleetwood FC having gone bust and been replaced by a new 1997 company. Steve eventually became assistant manager when Micky Mellon was appointed manager and enjoyed promotion success before leaving football to concentrate full-time on his physiotherapy business; a service I avail myself of from time to time.

I had been training the Fleetwood Car Centre team for a bit before I began turning out for them on the odd occasion when they were short and my knees would allow it.

Steve Abbott had a contact in the car industry in a bloke called Larry, who ran a Ford franchise and who was also heavily involved in amateur football in the Republic of Ireland. So, what could be more natural than a footballing tour of Ireland as the guests of Larry and his friends?

Our first Irish trip took place in 1996 and led to a string of low-level international competitions between the two outfits that went on for ten consecutive years. On our first trip to Dublin we played a team called Bangor City, which was a bit baffling as Bangor is in Northern Ireland.

Whatever their origins, Bangor were a good team and the initial intention was to arrive on the Friday, play a one-off game on the Saturday morning, have a few drinks, and then head for home.

We enjoyed that first trip so much that we decided to do it all over again the next year and it progressed from there. We started out playing eleven a side games, but as the years rolled on, and with lads coming and going, we ended up playing seven-a-side games. We never managed to beat the Bangor team, despite us having Steve Macauley in our ranks.

In Dublin we usually stayed in the lively Temple Bar area of the city, where we were unlikely to run out of pubs to frequent. It didn't matter whether a bar had karaoke or not, we always ended up singing. Songs from either side of the political divide in Ireland seemed equally welcome and there was one particular character who seemed to relish the singing more than most.

This lad's name was Rocky, and, as you might imagine, he had a reputation for being one of the toughest lads in Dublin, even though he was not very tall. On one occasion we were all singing and we were suddenly joined by this big Sikh fella, complete with brightly coloured turban. I don't know what the Sikh was singing and neither did anybody else, all I do know is, that during a brief pause for breath, Rocky jumped up and filled the silence with, "Doo, wah, diddy, diddy dum, diddy, doo!"

This brought the house down. And that was when the fun really started. We started challenging people to do ridiculous things and if they could not come up with the goods, then they had to do a forfeit. One of them involved a whole bucket of water being emptied down Rocky's trousers. He was furious about this, threatening death and all kinds of mayhem to his team-mates.

In one pub we set up an England versus Ireland tournament in a game that went like this. Two lads were blindfolded and given a dessert spoon that they had to hold in their mouths. Each lad had to then whack the other lad on the head with the spoon - the idea being that the damage would not be too great, what with the spoon being held in the mouth. However, we had set one of our lads up.

This lad was called Stewart, and what he didn't know was that every time it was his turn to be bashed by the Irish spoon holder, what actually happened was that Steve Macauley snuck up behind him and gave him a bloody great whack on the head with a ladle. Stewart howled with pain every time he got whacked with the ladle, but with the lads cheering him on from the side lines, he didn't feel as if he could quit. "Come on, Stewart! This is for England!" they would yell as the ladle came crashing down. In the end he ended up with a head like a watermelon. He totally failed to see the funny side of it, although the same could not be said of the assembled spectators, who were just about pissing themselves laughing.

In an echo of my childhood football career, I found myself playing in goal. If the ground was soft, it was alright and I could play and dive around as necessary, but if the ground was hard and I feared that my knee was going to take a battering, then I wouldn't bother diving. I would just let the shots in. One wag compared me to Alan Rough.

During all these trips to Ireland the craic was fierce. One of our number was a big local lad called Dave Burns. Apart from having the driest sense of humour you could imagine, Dave is also one of the nicest people you could ever meet.

One day we were walking along O'Connell Street and came to the bridge that crosses the River Liffey. As we were walking over the bridge a bloke pulled up alongside us in fancy dress. I said to him, "Fucking hell, you look well!" Whereupon, he jumped straight off the bridge and into the river. This prompted Dave Burns to remark, "Fuck me, Derek, you only spoke to him for a second and now he has gone and committed suicide!" I have never laughed so much in my life. I hope the bloke managed to get out of the river.

Even when the European Championship finals were on and we were all decked out in England football gear, we never experienced any animosity. It seemed that most of the Irish people we met were also rooting for England. The only negative incident was when Steve Macauley's dad and a mate of his strayed into a bar where anti-English feeling was particularly high. Somebody sidled over to them and quietly suggested that when they finished their drinks, they might prefer to find another watering hole. But apart from this one little problem, we were well treated by everybody we met.

Chapter 20 [1997]

A new relationship and a trip to America - Life is good

I eventually ended up staying for five years in the little flat on Heathfield Road in Fleetwood. Not the most salubrious area or the most sought-after postcode in Lancashire, but I come from a council estate in Belfast and settled in with no problems. I felt comfortable in that environment as I have never felt very at ease in the company of what you might call middle-class people. Or posh twats as my Daddy might have said.

I was financially secure, and with a few tenants all paying their rent to me, things weren't too bad.

Life takes some funny turns. I was not expecting to meet and fall in love with somebody 20 years my junior. But that is exactly what happened. Lyn and I had lots in common: our love of sport, music and a shared sense of humour. Even though Lyn and I had known each other since 1988, through my time at the off license in Hambleton, the extent of our relationship until 1997 had been that of employer and employee. But the more time I spent with her, the closer I felt to her and eventually we became more than just good friends as they say in the gossip columns.

Lyn had joined Blackpool's Football in the Community scheme in the August of 1997; the idea being that she helped-out with the day to day running of the scheme. The Oyston family let me get on with things in my own way although the cynic in me would opine that this was because they had no interest in our work whatsoever. The only times they were supportive was when gates were low when they handed us an ample supply of free tickets to hand out to local schools etc.

Mind you, when things were going well and Blackpool were at Wembley or in the Premier League, tickets became more elusive than Lord Lucan, and despite the fact that part of our role was to promote Blackpool FC in the community, Lyn and I had to pay for our own tickets when the club reached two play-off finals during Ian Holloway's reign as manager. Indeed, during the Premier League season, we bought our own season tickets.

I reported to director Chris Muir and enjoyed a fantastic relationship with him.

Different managers came and went and some of them I got on with and some of them I didn't. Steve McMahon was a particular bete noire, not just for me but virtually everyone. But I learnt to take the rough with the smooth and enjoyed myself.

It was whilst working with the Football in The Community programme that Lyn and I coached a girls' football team from Collegiate High School in Blackpool. There was a national tournament that led the way to an international competition, both of which were heavily sponsored by Adidas. To get to the international phase, it was necessary to win your country's national phase of the competition, so the chances of winning were slim. The prize for the winning team was an all-expenses paid trip to New York to attend the opening ceremony of the Women's World Cup, which was to be held at the Giants' Stadium across the river in New Jersey.

For us to have any chance of getting to the national final, I was going to have to take my coaching duties seriously. But once I had seen these girls play, I started to think we were in with a chance. All of them were pretty good players. The captain was a girl called Rachel Duncan, who was five feet ten inches tall. She led by example and was an outstanding central defender in the Nemanja Vidic mould. Her teammates were all comfortable on the ball and the goalkeeper was as fearless as Bert Trautman. Apart from Rachel, the team was a bit on the diminutive side, and I was worried that this was one factor that might work against them. As it turned out I need not have worried.

To cut a long story short, our team sailed through to the finals of the competition, in which the best team from the north faced the best team from the south at Wembley.

The day of the final was an emotional one. The Collegiate girls travelled down by coach and stayed at a hotel near Wembley on the eve of the big game. On the morning they were starting to feel nervous and as kick-off approached you could sense their trepidation.

It was up to me to bring my experience of playing in big games to bear and to calm them down with some wise words. Lyn took the girls out onto the sacred turf of Wembley, where they got their first look at the opposition. The other team seemed to be a race of Amazons. They were all massive. The Collegiate girls started to doubt themselves. But once I had made an assessment of their playing skills by watching their warm-up drills, I came back to our camp with the good news. Girls, I said, if you don't beat this lot by five clear goals I will show my arse in Burton's window.

The girls got out on the pitch and within five minutes or so, it became obvious that the Collegiate team had nothing to worry about: they were superior in every department. They duly won the national tournament and that meant that they were on their way to the USA. Two members of staff from

Adidas came, as did a further two members of staff from Collegiate School.

Naturally, as head coach, I was on the trip and I had back up from another member of the Football in the Community staff, in the shape of Lyn. Surely six adults would be enough to cope with a group of innocent teenagers from Blackpool? But the very things that made them such formidable opponents on the pitch were the same qualities that made them 'challenging' to look after. They were fiery, brave and independently minded. It was like trying to herd cats.

The girls played two games against American opposition, which they won, but these games were much closer, as the Americans were pretty skilful.

The highlight of the trip was undoubtedly the opening ceremony of the Women's World Cup. It became obvious that somewhere behind us a celebrity lurked. It was none other than Pelé. Two of the girls decided to get a closer look and they moved back along the rows of seats, forcing other people to squeeze up to accommodate them. Their goal was to get a photo of them together with the great man. I don't know how they achieved it, but they managed to get their photo. Two girls from Blackpool daintily perched on the knee of the somewhat bewildered Brazilian legend.

Another thing that sticks in the mind was a trip to Central Park, where Adidas had a football themed event. The singer and actress, Billie Piper was there, and she made a special effort to come over and have a chat with her compatriots. It was a great experience and Adidas were very generous sponsors. Each of the girls came back with an enormous goodie bag filled to the brim with Adidas sports gear.

All in all, a supremely memorable occasion.

Chapter 21 [1998]
The 'Troubles' and the 1998 Good Friday Agreement - Peace at last?

Sportsmen and women - if they are to be successful - have to be totally focused on their sport.

They invariably rely on their partners to solve the day to day problems at home and are often largely oblivious to anything happening in the outside world that is non-sport related. During my football career, I too was guilty of living a similarly blinkered life. I lived in a bubble as I attempted to make as big a success of my career as I could.

I have already mentioned the impact my career had on my first marriage, but it also impacts on your wider family. Ever since leaving Northern Ireland in 1970, I kept in touch with my family back home, telephoning them regularly and visiting when I could. I followed the events in Ulster on the television and of course I worried about my family living in such a dangerous part of the world. Every time an atrocity happened, I would anxiously telephone my parents, siblings and other family members to make sure they were safe.

But all too often - as is demanded by your employer - football came first, second and third and it was not until I quit the game and returned to something akin to a normal life that I realised the full horror of 'The Troubles' and how those years had affected my family living in Belfast.

The Good Friday Agreement (GFA) was welcomed by the majority of both communities in Ulster. The nationalist Paramilitary IRA (PIRA) and their loyalist counterparts, the Ulster Defence Association (UDA) and Ulster Volunteer Force (UVF), had agreed to a ceasefire, and after protracted talks between the various political parties, the GFA was implemented, restoring self-government to Northern Ireland on a power-sharing basis.

In 1999 an executive was formed consisting of the four main political parties, including Sinn Fein and the Democratic Unionist Party (DUP) led by Ian Paisley. The Royal Ulster Constabulary was re-formed, and re-named as the Police Service of Northern Ireland, and the abolition of 'Diplock' Courts signalled a normalisation of the legal process.

Eventually, the British Army withdrew its forces and the paramilitary groups handed in at least some of their weapons as part of an agreed amnesty.

Thankfully, the peace has largely held and, whilst a degree of sectarian violence is still an unfortunate part of life in Ulster, there can be no doubt that life for the majority of the population has improved immeasurably. Peace and the regeneration of Belfast has led to something of a tourist boom and people largely now live a normal life, free from the terrors of the past.

When I left Belfast in 1970, the 'Troubles', which had largely lain dormant for several decades, were beginning to burst back into life. Just prior to my departure for England, riots had broken out in 1969, leading to the deployment of British Troops who built so called 'Peace Walls' to keep the respective communities apart. I was lucky inasmuch that I was destined to miss the worst of the Northern Ireland conflict from 1970 onwards.

The conflict was primarily political and nationalistic, fuelled by historic events. Many people on mainland Britain believed that the main source of divergence was religion, but whilst it cannot be denied that the two communities were largely split along religious lines, it is too simplistic to attribute it to religious faith alone. Not all Catholics are nationalists/republicans and not all Protestants are unionists/loyalists. Indeed, briefly, the UDA toyed with the idea of Northern Ireland becoming an independent country, so angry were sections of the loyalist community about the role of the British Government during the conflict.

In essence, the 'Troubles' was a tussle between two communities. One community (the nationalists/ republicans) favouring a united Ireland whilst the loyalist/unionists insisted that Northern Ireland not only remained a separate entity to the Republic of Ireland but also continued to be wedded to Great Britain and the British monarchy. Inevitably, therefore, the divide was largely between Catholics and Protestants. As a result, sectarian violence, between communities who for many years previously had largely lived in peaceful co-existence, accelerated alarmingly. Indeed, a form of ethnic cleansing took shape with minority groups leaving one area to move to towns where they felt safer. Almost overnight, Northern Ireland became more divided than ever before with previously mixed areas of residence becoming almost exclusively Protestant or Catholic.

Tit for tat killings became common and whilst England was more fixated on outrages linked to the PIRA's bombing of mainland British targets, Northern Ireland's population faced far more frequent horrors, living as they were in what was effectively a war-torn state.

More than 3,500 people were killed in the Northern Ireland conflict, of whom 52% were civilians, 32% members of the British security forces, and 16% associated to some degree or another with paramilitary groups. There has been sporadic violence since the GFA was signed, including a campaign by anti-ceasefire republicans, but thankfully, at the time of writing, the peace still holds and, Brexit related concerns aside, the future of the country looks bright.

I was elated when the GFA was signed and it has been wonderful to see on my now more frequent trips home how the country has adjusted to peace, with a generation of youngsters having lived only in non-violent times.

By 1998 I had been retired from football for many years and, with the security and stability provided by my job with the Blackpool FC Trust, I now had more time to dwell on the 'Troubles' and, in particular, the impact it had on my family.

Probably because they wanted to protect me at the time and not cause me unnecessary worry, I discovered that many family members had a story to tell that I knew little or nothing about. I realised with perfect clarity how my life in England had saved me from such horrors and I even felt guilty about previously bitching about the occasional abuse I had received from Englishmen about my Irish roots every time a PIRA atrocity took place on the mainland.

My sister, Isabella, during the time her husband Aubrey owned the O'Hara Bakery, was caught up in an armed raid when she and several employees were held captive by gunmen. Mercifully, no-one was killed (for reasons we still cannot fathom) and my sister escaped but I still feel somewhat haunted even today by how close to death she came.

I have had family members robbed at knifepoint, my Daddy was frequently in danger due to his work and the places it took him to, and my kid brother, Alex, suffered some terrible experiences as the troubles intensified infinitely, although he still insists that he had a brilliant childhood!

In the early days of the 'Troubles', like most Protestant kids, Alex had many Catholic friends. That is if he knew what religion they were because in most instances back then, only the real zealots cared that much. He played in a mixed football team managed by Paul Byrne and got on with pretty much everybody.

When aged 13, he witnessed the shooting of a policeman at a Crusaders game in 1980. Alex was standing just yards away from the incident as it happened.

As a kid, it was normal for Alex to see the Army 'sweeping' the streets and as the tensions grew, he was exposed to more and more horror. Not long after the Crusaders killing, he was looking after a neighbour's son who was playing on his bike. The kid in question had made several laps of the block when suddenly he didn't re-emerge. Alex went to look for him and discovered that some local Catholic kids had pushed the youngster off his bike, for no other reason than that he was a "Proddie".

Alex tore into the kids and gave them a pummelling. Not long afterwards, the father of one of the kids' caught up with Alex and battered him. The bloke was a well-known local Provo but that didn't bother our Daddy and by all accounts, within minutes of him learning about the attack on his son, Daddy had returned the compliment. And some. According to Alex, Daddy didn't even speak, he just started hitting the bloke until he slumped to the ground. Daddy had always nicknamed Alex the "Astronaut" but that day it was Daddy that rocketed into action.

A couple of years later, a close pal of Alex was beaten to death outside his house when some local catholic lads spotted him drunkenly trying to find his door key.

After that, Alex was never out of trouble and in desperation Daddy asked me to get him to England so that he could start a new life.

My brother was particularly close to Mummy as, due to him being so much younger than the rest of us, she had basically brought him up alone without any other children to worry about by then. So, leaving home was going to be a huge wrench.

In 1983 he briefly joined me in Southend. Aged 15, and by now a talented footballer, he joined in with training and later, accompanied by Daddy, had trials with both Manchester City and Manchester United. Whilst with United, and training at the Cliff, he was routinely greeted in a friendly manner by those senior players that knew him through me. His fellow triallists looked on aghast as he happily exchanged banter with the likes of Jimmy Nicholl, Sammy McIlroy and David McCreery.

But the incidents back in Belfast had affected him badly and certainly interfered with his football to the point that he gave the game up. Despite his talent, he was never offered a pro deal and over time gradually fell out of love with football. He continually suffered from flashbacks, night terrors, anxiety attacks, etc, and even when he later came to live with me in Bury he still couldn't put the past behind him and was frequently in fights around the town. He used to suffer from incandescent rages that could only be quelled by fighting. It would be another 20 years before finally, after an incident in a park when he became enraged by a minor incident involving his son, he went for counselling.

I love Alex to bits and thankfully the counselling has worked wonders. He has a fabulous family and now returns to Northern Ireland for brief visits largely at peace with himself and his traumatic past.

Alex and his wife Michelle tell a funny story relating to the first time he took Michelle to Belfast to meet his family during the 'Troubles'. One night, they decided to go out for a meal and drinks to a place out of town. Alex drove them and within minutes they were stopped at an Army roadblock. Alex brought the car to an immediate halt and after answering a few questions from the armed patrolmen, drove off totally unfazed.

However, all this was new to Michelle, a scouser who had lived in England all her life, and even when minutes later they sat down for their meal, she remained traumatised by what she had just witnessed. In fact, so upset was she, Alex felt compelled to take her back home to his parents house without ordering any food. Their night out had lasted 30 minutes all told, and Daddy apparently wetted himself as they related the story to him. He laughed even more furiously when Michelle explained that her distress had been heightened further when she later realised that if she'd have been driving she would unquestionably have refused to stop and driven straight through the barricade in a blind panic. A tale that surely emphasises vividly what for one person was totally normal, was terrifyingly out of the ordinary for another.

Daddy lived in Belfast throughout his life and to the best of our knowledge only considered leaving once. The suspicion remains that his change of mind was influenced by the fact he was behind with his rent payments, but he did love Belfast and I'm sure that was foremost in his thinking.

So respected was he by people on both sides of the divide, that on the day of his funeral, hundreds of people stood outside the house in quiet tribute. The UVF, UDA and PIRA were all represented and even followed the cortege to the bottom of Serpentine Road.

Daddy was respected for many reasons. He was a hard man and took no shit, but he was a good man too who would do jobs (without reward) for anyone regardless of their religion or political beliefs. He remained aloof to the 'Troubles' and stubbornly refused to allow the conflict taking place on his doorstep to interfere with his day to day life. Sometimes putting himself in greater jeopardy as a result.

If Daddy wanted to go out or drive to a certain place, then he would. No terrorist was going to stop him doing what he either wanted or needed to do. On one occasion, whilst I was still married to Frances, we, Daddy and some of his mates were having a drink in the social club at Crusaders FC. He had just ordered another round when an alarm went off signifying a bomb alert.

We were all told to leave immediately, and Frances was on the verge of dragging my hand away from my arm, so frantically was she tugging at my appendage, willing me to take her to sanctuary outside. How did Daddy react? "Bollocks to it, I'm going nowhere" he thundered. And he didn't. He stayed put, finished his pint and, on learning soon afterwards that the security forces had confirmed the incident to be a false alarm, barracked us unmercifully for our `cowardice'.

Daddy coached boxing at the local club and although he loved football, boxing was undoubtedly his favourite sport. It brought him into contact with all sections of the two communities, and as he didn't charge anybody a penny for the training, his popularity grew. He rarely holidayed, although he did visit me in Greece when I was with Olympiacos, bringing Alex with him. They even travelled to an away game on the coach. Daddy was a home bird though and remained so no matter how serious the problems he and his community faced.

There are numerous, momentous and tragic events of the 'Troubles' that I could recount but I don't think this book is the place to do that. The Northern Ireland conflict is now a subject for history books and hopefully a part of the history of Ulster which will never be repeated.

I have always been a moderate man politically and although I got into the odd scrape or two as a kid - incidents which would now be regarded as sectarian in nature, I never thought of myself as a signed-up unionist/loyalist. I believe in God but I am genuinely not bothered - and never was - what religious faith a person follows. I simply want my fellow countrymen to lead peaceful and happy lives and as I enter my late 60's I remain thrilled by the fact that I lived to see peace restored in my home country and that I can now rest at ease, not worrying about the safety of loved ones back home.

Just recently, I revisited Northern Ireland with a friend who has helped me write this book. Our story is at Chapter 29.

Chapter 22 [2002]

A death and a birth

For four years my life had been relatively plain sailing. I continued to work for the Blackpool FC Trust and both Lyn and I were enjoying the challenge of what was proving to be both a fulfilling and enjoyable role.

I even had a brief spell coaching one of the Blackpool FC academy teams after Wayne Harrison was offered the job of Head Academy Coach and persuaded me to work for him on a part-time basis. As I anticipated, coaching was not for me but at least I gave it a go.

But life is full of ups and downs and no year summed that up more aptly than 2002.

In May, Lyn and I celebrated our first child together when she gave birth to our son, Thomas. We were overjoyed and I was ecstatic about being a father again.

In September, Lyn and I were holidaying blissfully with baby Thomas at Centre Parks in Nottingham when I received a telephone call saying that my mother had been rushed to hospital and was seriously ill.

I immediately took the Holyhead to Dublin ferry and then drove to Belfast, all the time hoping against hope that either it was a false alarm or that I would at least get to say a last goodbye to my dear old Mummy.

When I arrived at the hospital, she was on a life support machine and very poorly. She had suffered a bad fall and had been found by a neighbour.

My brother and sisters were already there, and we were soon joined by the vicar, a female member of the clergy called Alice. She led us in a recital of the Lord's Prayer and then, after a consultation with the doctors followed by a traumatic family discussion, we made the decision to switch the life machine off. The staff had made it clear that there was no chance of Mummy recovering and that the kindest gesture was to end her suffering with dignity.

I remained by Mummy's bed after the machine had been switched off determined to remain by her side until she drew her last breath. She was on morphine and at eight am I finally succumbed and took a break. Just half an hour later she died.

I was heartbroken, not just because she had passed away but because she had gone without my presence alongside her. One of my few consolations was that she had at least seen Thomas before she had passed.

I loved my Mummy. She was a good woman and mother and she enjoyed being a grandmother to my kids. After my father's death, she had coped surprisingly well, seemingly gaining a new lease of life. She found new companions and enjoyed the final years of her life to the full.

As alluded to several times, Mummy spent virtually her whole married life in the kitchen. I hope she enjoyed it. She was certainly gifted in that respect and the family still recall her gorgeous angel buns with awe.

Like many of the Spence family, particularly my sister Isabella, Mummy loved singing and was very talented but, sadly, she was an extremely shy woman and was reticent about singing in public which was a great shame. Needless to say, the other members of the Spence clan have no such difficulty about singing in public, although to be fair we lack her talent.

Like many women back then, Mummy rarely went to watch me play. Like my Daddy, she was a home-bird happiest at home busying herself in the plethora of tasks generated by a big family. Unlike Daddy, she wasn't a drinker although, surprisingly perhaps, she enjoyed playing darts at the local social club.

Mummy was generally a calm woman, although she most certainly had a fierce temper when roused, as Daddy could have testified. Family legend has it that when visiting you could work out that weeks' meals by the traces on the wallpaper of whatever dish had been thrown by either of them during a row.

No doubt about it though, she was a great mother and on the day of her funeral, all the family were there to say goodbye to her.

Chapter 23 (2003)

Derek gets spliced for a second time - Nuptials

Once I had finally plucked up the courage, Lyn and I got married in 2003 in Yorkshire. In the build up to our engagement, I took her away to London. I had planned to ask for her hand in a swanky restaurant but there were too many people sat near the table and, full of nerves, I got drunk and therefore postponed the task until we had returned to our hotel.

Thankfully, she said yes and whilst in London I bought her an engagement ring.

My sister-in-law, Leslie lived in Hull and her husband, Brian, had been diagnosed with throat cancer in 2002 and so, as it looked like he didn't have long to live, Lyn and I decided to go over and see them.

We set off on a Friday night and, as we had not booked any accommodation, we were frantically ringing round trying to find somewhere to stay. Eventually we found a place in Wakefield: not really that convenient when you want to be in Hull, but it was the best we could do at short notice.

The place we stayed at was called Waterton Park Hotel. It was a big manor house with a lake complete with an island in the middle. When we got up on the Saturday morning we saw that they had a wedding on that day and we also saw how lovely it all looked with the bridge that led to the island all decked out with bunting and ribbons.

We managed to see Brian before he died. Even though he was on Frances' side of the family we had always got on well, the split from Frances not seeming to affect our relationship.

Although the circumstances behind our finding the venue were extremely sad, Lyn and I decided that Waterton Park Hotel would make the ideal venue for our nuptials. We got married in the December of 2003 and at the time of writing we have been married for almost 16 years and have two children together; Thomas, who was born in May 2002 before we tied the knot, and Erin, who came along three years later in the May of 2005.

I always feel a bit guilty about my eldest son, Matthew, from my first marriage. He was a very talented footballer, who played for Northern Ireland at under 18 level, and I am sure that without all the emotional turmoil in his life at the time of the divorce, he would have gone on to make a career in the game. But he took a year out of the game, and by the time he came back to it, the fire had gone out a bit.

Despite us all going through some pretty hard times together we have come out on the other side of it all with a great deal of mutual love and respect. I have a great relationship with both of them and love them with all my heart. They have never caused me a moment's concern and happily both get on well with Lyn and their younger stepbrother and sister.

The break-up of my first marriage caused me a great deal of heartache and soul searching, but these days it seems that fragmented and fractured families are the norm, rather than the exception, and I take some comfort from the fact that lots of my contemporaries have been through broadly similar experiences. A few years ago it might have been the norm to stay in a marriage or relationship that was going nowhere - perhaps for the sake of the children - but I did not want to see myself in that situation.

The day of my second wedding was great. Family and friends came from all the places where I had relatives or friends. There was a contingent from Northern Ireland and one from Hull and a few people made their way up from Essex.

For our honeymoon we went to Mexico. We even went to that bloody big pyramid at Chichen Itsa, but I didn't climb to the top of the thing, as I didn't think my knees were up to it. I loved everything about Mexico, especially the people.

Chapter 24 [2004-2009]
Jimmy Nicholl comes calling - But I stay with Blackpool

Lyn and I made our marital home in Fleetwood and we have lived there ever since.

In 2004 Billy Bingham left his job as manager of the Northern Ireland team and that left a vacancy at the top of the footballing pyramid in my home country. One Sunday morning I got a phone call from my old pal Jimmy Nicholl, who was due to be interviewed for the vacancy a couple of days later. Jimmy looked pretty much nailed on for the job, as he had worked with Bingham previously and his appointment could be a viewed as a kind of succession.

At that time Jimmy was working in Scotland, where he had been doing very well, taking lowly Raith Rovers into Europe and then going on to the manager's job at Dunfermline. Jimmy was looking for an assistant manager and out of all the people he could have phoned, he chose to call me. Just to be considered for such a post was an honour.

The problem for me was that my knee was in a real mess due to the accumulated effect of various playing injuries. Later on I went on to have a knee replacement operation, which improved my mobility considerably, but prior to the op, I was hobbling. I could not see myself running up and down the line coaching the national squad in warm-up sessions, which would have been a part of my duties.

For a few days I was on tenterhooks whilst this situation resolved itself. Even though Jimmy was regarded as being a certainty for the job, in the end he missed out to Lawrie Sánchez, formerly of Wimbledon FC's crazy gang. Rumour had it that Jimmy priced himself out of the job with excessive financial demands. However, nothing could be further from the truth. Jimmy had already accepted, in principle, a drop of around 30% in wages, but when push came to shove the Northern Ireland FA was keen for him to take another drop in salary if they were to give him the job. At that point it became obvious that for Jimmy to take the national job would have been a form of economic suicide.

I know that Jimmy must have been gutted to have missed out on the chance to manage his country. From a purely selfish point of view, I was disappointed that I could not renew my ties and friendship with the man I had roomed with for seven years during our time together in the national squad. I was also, if truth be told, a bit relieved, as the assistant manager's role is a high-pressure one. Who knows how things would have turned out if Jimmy had accepted the job and I had gone to work for him as his right-hand man. On the other hand, had my career gone in that direction, I would not have had the chance to develop my role promoting football in the community.

It was back then to the grindstone in my job as Blackpool FC's Community Officer. Essentially, my job was to bring money into this stand-alone project: the money does not go to the football club. This was a high-pressure role in its own right. Although I was paid a salary, as the job is self-funding, the continuing payment of that salary depends upon one thing: my ability to bring money in. As you can imagine, this could be extremely stressful at times.

For many years Blackpool FC has been in the hands of the Oyston family. Family patriarch Owen Oyston is well known as a self-made millionaire with interests in the property and printing industries. His champagne socialist lifestyle attracted a fair bit of attention in the press at both local and national levels. His habit of attending matches in a Malcolm Allison-style fedora meant he was rarely out of the news.

He also had a well-publicised brush with the law a few years ago and served some time at Her Majesty's pleasure. As a consequence, Owen passed the day to day running of the club to his son, Karl, who, it is fair to say, had his fair share of critics.

Another well-known local businessman with a keen eye on Blackpool FC is David Haythornthwaite, who made his money in the animal and veterinary supplies industry. It was an open secret that David wanted to buy the club, but he and Karl Oyston did not exactly see eye to eye, which was why my heart was in my mouth when I asked Karl for permission to approach his local rival in an attempt to raise some funds for the community project.

I received permission and duly went to see Mr Haythornthwaite. As any funds I raised were kept separate from the football club, I was able to come away from that particular meeting with a very healthy £40,000 donation, enabling me to approach the government so that they could match the figure under the Sports Match programme. I was very grateful to David Haythornthwaite and his company, Tangerine Holdings. Their donation was vital to our cause and allowed us to do so many positive things in the years ahead.

The Fylde Coast is lucky to have several benefactors who donate their time and money to local football. Fleetwood Town was bought by one such football minded entrepreneur a few years ago and under the leadership of energy industry guru and ex-Blackpool supporter, Andy Pilley, the Cod Army - as they are known locally - have gone from playing in the North West Counties League in front of less than 100 spectators to the third tier of English football. Arguably the most incredible rags to riches football story of all time.

As I have lived in Fleetwood for a number of years now, I consider myself an honorary 'Cod Head' and support Fleetwood Town almost as much as I support my former clubs.

As for David Haythornwaite, his football ambitions were finally realised when he later took control of AFC Fylde who are now a top National League outfit with a pristine new stadium and ambitions of entering the football league in the not too distant future.

My role with the community scheme gave me the chance to meet quite a few high-profile people, both locally and nationally. One of my best allies was the local MP, Joan Humble, who helped me enormously. Right from the off, Joan understood that football has the transformative power to reach out and change lives for the better. She was our conduit to the Government, backing up our message that investment in football related programmes would reap benefits with regard to young people getting involved in sport, taking up exercise and generally leading more active lives.

Eventually the Football in the Community programme morphed into something a lot more complex. For quite a while I was answerable to Blackpool FC director Chris Muir, who had previously been a director at Manchester City. He was massively supportive with regards to everything I did and relayed all the good news back up the chain to his fellow directors.

When Chris died, which was a massive blow to all of us at the club, Karl Oyston appointed local retired businessman

Gavin Steele to oversee the Football in the Community project, along with the School of Excellence.

Things were about to change radically for me. Eventually the Football League took over the community side of things and for a while it looked as if I was going to be shown the door. However, with Gavin Steele lobbying on my behalf, I was able to ride out the storm and emerge on the other side of it with a new role in a very different set up.

That left just Lyn and me to spearhead this new challenge. Eventually it was decided that we should set up a charitable trust. Much of our work under this new scheme would be dealing with requests for funding and the way forward was to find projects that were financed by such bodies as the NHS, the Prince's Trust and various local government agencies. For quite a few years we were the biggest deliverers of a project called "Get started with football" under the auspices of the Prince's Trust.

This provided us with plenty of experience of working with young adults who were deemed to be at risk of offending. After the original Football in the Community scheme, which was set up and based at the PFA offices in Manchester, ceased to exist in 2007, the running of all football club community schemes was taken over by the Football League Trust and the community schemes came under the Football League Banner.

This outcome met with mixed feelings for me, as I had made some good friends in the offices in Manchester, who then had to move on to new roles. Roger Reade, who had been the Chief executive of the Football in the Community Scheme, Dennis Leman, ex Manchester City player and Deputy Chief Executive and John Hudson, an ex-Oldham player, was given the role of North West Regional Manager, at the same time I had been given the job at Blackpool. He was responsible for supporting all the North West clubs including Blackpool.

Over the eleven years that John and I worked together we became good friends and still remain close to this day. He is now the Director of Corporate Responsibility at the PFA and still works alongside Denis Leman, I really enjoyed keeping in touch and working with such valuable friends and colleagues.

When the Football League got involved it meant massive changes and growth in Blackpool's participation in the scheme.

With the guidance and support of Regional Manager, Dean Grice - who has become a valued friend to both Lyn and me, things went from strength to strength. The involvement of the Football League meant that we were able to access bigger and better funding to support and develop different projects. We were able to employ more staff to work on some of these projects.

2009 saw the birth of the new "Blackpool FC Community Trust", with Lyn overseeing the granting of charitable status. Five trustees were appointed and their sole responsibility was to look after the affairs of the trust. Gavin Steele was given the role of Chairman.

The Football League implemented a new structure, with clubs accessing different levels of funding according to their level of accreditation. These levels were Bronze, Silver and Gold. All clubs reached the required Bronze and Blackpool achieved Silver status in 2009, which meant extra funds were now available allowing us to progress even further and positively impact yet more young lives.

Through my role at the club, I was able to meet some rather important people. Among the numerous politicians I met were, Tony Blair, Michael Ancram and John Prescott. After meeting them, I realised just what a funny bunch many politicians are: all smiles when the cameras are on them, but cold as ice once they think the photo opportunity has passed by....... with the exception of Blair, who came across as a genuinely nice bloke. Nowadays, because of his role in the Iraq War fiasco, he is a hate figure for many but I can only speak as I find. The day I met him he impressed me enormously and I really warmed to him.

John Prescott was the best of the bunch though, and he came to see us at Fleetwood when for some reason I was given the role of showing the deputy PM round some new footballing facilities at a secondary school in town. For reasons best known to himself, Mr Prescott decided to join in with an informal kickabout that was taking place. He had played a bit of football as a youngster and looked quite useful. He even skinned a couple of young lads and went past them down the wing, complete with business suit, shiny brogues and smart tie.

But he had reckoned without the defensive zeal of one of our young lads. This kid was, to put it mildly, a bit competitive and he had decided that no politician was going to glide past him. A steely glare transfixed his features and as the second most powerful politician in the country prepared to make it a hat-trick of bemused defenders, the lad struck. He came flying in with a challenge that had malice aforethought written all over it. Prescott went up in the air and came down face first in the mud, business suit and all.

But credit where credit is due, he gamely picked himself up, dusted himself off and got on with the game. He even had a smile on his face. Unfortunately, no pictures exist. Perhaps just as well as Mr Prescott's political career was set to take a major turn for the worse anyway not long afterwards when his private life became the subject of lurid tabloid exclusives.

A year or so later I got a call from Labour Party headquarters at Millbank. Would I be prepared to accompany a certain VIP on a trip to the Trades Club in Blackpool? This was at the time of the Labour Party's annual conference in the town. Naturally, I said yes. It seemed that my role in this was to be a local guide accompanying this big wig: but who could it be? Very little fuss had been made when Mr Prescott came up.

I started to suspect that it would be my job to squire none other than Prime Minister, Tony Blair. That was when I started to get nervous. In fact, I was beyond nervous: I was bloody terrified. Subsequently, the PM's office confirmed that it was indeed Tony Blair that they had been referring to all along. They provided me with the notes for a long speech, which I had to read out, with the names of various cabinet ministers and other politicians; all of whom had to be thanked for their many and varied contributions to the party cause. I have never been much of a one for reading and the more I practised saying these names, the more I mangled them. The more I worried, the more I practised and the more I practised the more of a mess I made. Come the day itself, I was shitting myself.

I was taken into this dingy backroom where a little fella, who turned out to be a Scottish trade union official, was waiting for me alongside a very tall bloke: Tony Blair. He towered over me as he shook my hand and asked me what team I had played for. I was so nervous that I blurted out, "Man United!" When I realised what I had said, I knew that

I had to rectify matters, and so I supplied the desperate addendum, "In my dreams!" Eventually, I managed to relax a bit and come up with a few words of common sense and truth, as I told him that I had played with George Best, even if I had never been a regular first teamer at the Theatre of Dreams.

Thankfully, my attack of nerves had the effect of acting like an ice breaker and after a minute or so I calmed down. Once I had relaxed, we went round to the Trades Club and I introduced my mate Tone to all the local party members and activists. We had pictures taken and then it was time for me to do my speech and the nerves came back with a vengeance. I started reading the list of all the people I had to thank and I came across a name I couldn't pronounce and I just froze.

So I did the only thing I could do under the circumstances: I omitted any name I didn't like the look of. I went on to the next page and in the end there must have been loads of people whose names I left out, but nobody seemed to realise or care.

Tony Blair eventually took his turn at the lectern and he went out of the way to show his appreciation, saying, "I would like to thank Derek Spence for showing me around today. And did you know? He used to play with George Best!"

I felt about ten feet tall. I still have the signed picture of Tony Blair with me and the rest of my family as a proud memento of the day I escorted the Prime Minister.

Chapter 25 (2005)
Death of a legend - Bestie - and another daughter

A footballing trip to Dublin in May 2005 gave me the chance to renew my acquaintance with my old pal and teammate, George Best. At Dublin airport, one of the lads (I think it was Wayne Brewer, brother in law of Steve Macauley) saw Bestie as he was about to go through the departure gate for an outbound flight.

The lad told George that I was with the party, but as he was in a rush, I never managed to get a word with him. He did pass on his phone number, however, and from then onwards we were in regular contact. Unfortunately, although we exchanged numerous texts, we were never to meet again face to face.

Best's untimely death in the November of 2005 came as quite a shock; even to those of us who were aware of the fragile state of his health.

His battle with the bottle has been well documented and needs no further comment from me. I prefer to remember a friend, a loyal team-mate and one of the greatest footballers the world has ever seen.

His funeral, which took place at Stormont Castle in Belfast, was virtually a state funeral. Free buses were laid on to take the thousands of mourners from the town centre out to Stormont. Manchester United fans from all over the world turned up to pay their respects to their legendary hero.

I had an invitation to attend the service inside the chapel itself, but decided, as I had Lyn with me and the invitation was for ex-players only, not their spouses, to take my place with the mourners outside. The gates opened at seven in the morning and we got there an hour earlier to say our goodbyes. At about half past nine the heavens opened and from then on we were treated to a proper Ulster-footballing-weather send-off.

The rain provided a commentary more eloquent than that supplied by any of the speakers on that sad day. Whenever I hear the song "Flying without wings" by Westlife, which they played on the day, I always think of the genius that was George Best.

It is strange the difference between ex-footballers and ordinary supporters. As a player, in the main, you don't really hate any player or football club. They are all rivals and although some rub you up more than others you don't feel any greater enmity for one more than another.

Of course, if you are playing in a derby match there is a special feeling and you do get caught up in the occasion and know it is a must-win game. And inevitably, poor experiences against an opponent mean there is an extra edge to it next time, but you don't necessarily hate anyone. For instance, although Billy Bingham broke my heart and I will never be able to forgive him, I did shake his hand we crossed paths for the first time when I returned to Blackpool in 1996 and he was a visitor at the ground one day.

I think Bestie was such a great player than even supporters of rival clubs admired him. However, my old Hambleton mate Paul Finnegan, a staunch Manchester City fan, is not one of them. When I once mentioned to him that I had been a team-mate and friend of George Best he recoiled in horror, stating that "He was the bloke (or words to that effect) who had broken Glyn Pardoe's leg". Although this had occurred many years ago in a long-forgotten early 70's derby match between the Manchester giants, Paul was still holding a grudge as is the wont of committed football fans.

Whilst a player at Bury I once attended a Manchester United game at Bolton Wanderers and didn't give a shit who won. I just fancied watching a game. I stood in the Bolton end and after a fine United move finished with the visitors scoring an excellent goal I made the mistake of applauding and opining "Great goal that, well played son". I soon regretted my audacious behaviour and actually had to leave the game early to escape the abuse and threats of violence.

People often say that they broke the mould when they made Bestie. I agree whole-heartedly and I think most football supporters would on balance concur and conclude that he was one of the all-time greats. Sorry, Paul, old mate.

Ironically, and happily, just as 2002 had marked the death of a key figure in my life but also the arrival of a much-loved child, so was the case in 2005 as Lyn and I welcomed the gorgeous Erin into our lives.

Chapter 26 [2009-2011]
The promised land - Blackpool hit the big time

At the end of the 2009/10 season Blackpool became the only British football team to have won promotion from every division of the Football League via the play-off system. Thanks almost entirely to Mr Ian Holloway.

The first time I ever met the sage of the West Country, I introduced myself to him as the club's community officer. I don't think anybody realised, initially, what a unique character Holloway was. The first time I got some inkling as to his talents was when I went down to the training ground to get some balls and shirts signed by the team for a charity auction. Ian had the lads passing like Barcelona at their best. All his work was around ball skills, possession and the quality of the passing. This approach stemmed from an enforced one-year sabbatical, when after being sacked by Leicester City after their relegation to the third tier, he flew off to Spain to do nothing but sit in the sun and absorb the special qualities of Spanish football.

At about this time I had had a gutful of football. I no longer enjoyed watching it or even talking about it. But the continental brand that Ian brought to Blackpool was a revelation. He admitted that, until his Spanish gap-year, much of his coaching had been based on fear: fear of losing and fear of losing possession. When he came back from Spain, he had, by all accounts, experienced an epiphany. Never again would one of his teams play with fear. They would play with verve, with brio and with panache.

Defensively they were a bit shaky, but bloody hell when a Holloway team was on the attack, you knew somebody was going to score, even if it was the opponents scoring on the break and putting the ball in the back of his team's net. The run in to the play-offs was a fabulous time for Blackpool and their fans. The secret to his success, apart from his habit of supplying the press with bizarre sound bites, was his ability to get the fans on board.

A key moment came when he gave a fierce bollocking to the fans in the hospitality suite, who were trying to enjoy their pre-match meal. Striker Jason Euell had been having a rough time of things and certain elements of the crowd were giving him stick every time he got anywhere near the ball. Holloway tore into Euell's critics and gave them a piece of his mind. He berated them, telling them it was their duty to get behind players, not to erode their confidence by continually slagging them off.

From then on, there was a different atmosphere about the club. The fans took his message to heart and every time the players went out on the pitch, they did so to the accompaniment of fans roaring them on to victory. To say that the season was an emotional roller coaster ride is an understatement. I can't remember any Blackpool team playing like that, apart, of course, from the team with Micky Walsh, Bob Hatton and me. Had there been a play-off system when that Blackpool team was playing, we too, might have gone on to win promotion to the top division, regardless of what it might have been called.

Once in the Premier League, Blackpool did themselves proud. They were still in with a chance of staying up on the final day of the season but had the misfortune to be playing Manchester United at Old Trafford, and so ended one of the most remarkable seasons in the club's history.

Despite having the Premier Leagues' most modest ever playing budget, Blackpool were a breath of fresh air. Unlike other promoted teams who invariably take the ultra-defensive approach, Blackpool attacked sides regardless of their stature. Relegation was no disgrace. Blackpool were one of the revelations of the campaign.

Holloway would subsequently lead Blackpool to another play-off final, this time losing out to Sam Allardyce's West Ham United.

Sadly, his time at Blackpool would end on a sour note and I still find it a mystery why he isn't remembered as a club legend.

Even more sadly, the deteriorating relationship between the Oyston family and Blackpool's fan base eventually led to many fans boycotting the club from 2015 until 2019. Gates sank to the thousand mark, boosted mainly by visiting supporters, and it was a common sight to see the boycotters outside the ground on match days effectively acting as pickets to dissuade those fans still paying to watch games from entering the stadium. Some fans were sued by the owners for social media libel, an absentee Blackpool director litigated against Owen Oyston for money he claimed he was owed and, finally, after a series of court cases, the last vestiges of the Oyston regime was removed by the Official Receiver in 2019 (as covered by my friend Steve Rowland in Chapter 31 of this book).

With the boycott over, I have again started watching Blackpool home games, an experience I really missed during those dark days. Hopefully, the club now has a bright future with Bloomfield Road again packed out.

I can't end this chapter without mentioning Jimmy Armfield. Legend is an overused word these days but Gentleman Jim was most certainly a Blackpool legend, as his statue outside Bloomfield Road confirms. Jimmy was a one club man, even turning down Matt Busby's Manchester

United, and he was a member of England's 1966 World Cup winning squad.

After retiring as a player, Jimmy managed Bolton Wanderers before, to the amazement of many, he accepted the poisoned chalice of being the Leeds United boss, replacing Brian Clough who had lasted just 44 days in the job. I often marvel at just how the mild-mannered, courteous Jimmy Armfield coped with powerful figures like Billy Bremner, Allan Clarke and Norman Hunter. But he clearly did a great job, quickly winning the respect of the dressing room, as their run to the 1975 European Cup Final proves.

After leaving Elland Road, Jimmy became a widely admired football summarizer on BBC Radio Five Live. Such was the respect for his knowledge of the game, the FA appointed him to recommend Graham Taylor's replacement as England manager, Jimmy ultimately opting for Terry Venables who was duly appointed in 1995.

In his capacity as Blackpool President, I came into contact with Jimmy on a regular basis whilst I was working for the Trust and he was immensely helpful to me.

He was a great, yet humble man and his death a couple of years ago was a very sad moment in my life.

Chapter 27 [2013-2016]

Retirement the second time - Derek picks up his bus pass

Blackpool's promotion to the Premier League was a fantastic boost for the scheme, not only through funding, but in general terms, as everyone wanted to be a part of anything to do with Blackpool FC. This made our jobs a lot easier.

I conducted motivational talks for young people who had lost their way in life, I put on coaching sessions in local schools with the aim of getting kids previously uninvolved in sporting activity playing football and even learning to coach and take their badges.

I ran holiday and Saturday football camps, undertook prison coaching sessions and generally immersed myself and the Trust in as much activity as possible, helping many vulnerable people in the process.

In 2013 there were further changes, with Gavin Steel resigning from his post as chairman of the Trust. This was a sad day for Lyn and me, as we had become good friends with both Gavin and his wife, Chris.

My role also changed: I became responsible for the National Citizen Service (NCS) Programme and the trustees brought in a new Head of Community to oversee the day to day running of the trust. I worked with youngsters of 16 and 17 in a role I found both challenging and rewarding. I was able to offer a lifetime of experience to young people who were at a very impressionable age.

This new project - a Government funded scheme - concentrated on teaching the importance of being part of a team within society. It was targeted at young people aged 15 to18, helping them to learn life skills. The Trust thought I was the right person to head this up and inspire young people from troubled backgrounds to make something more of their life. NCS included doing a two-week residential course, learning about the community and delivering a social action project including fund raising events and working with local charities.

I really enjoyed my new role, I was good at it too, working with over 700 young people in the Blackpool area. Hopefully, I gave these youngsters the confidence to move forward in life.

But, in the summer of 2016, at the ripe old age of 64, and after much deliberation, I made the decision to hang up my office shoes and retire from my role at the Trust, after serving the community for 20 years.

The Trust now has 40+ full time members of staff, working on projects as diverse as Soccer Schools, social inclusion, primary school health initiatives and sport for the over 55's to name just a few, so I feel I left a great legacy having started from scratch.

As a Northern Irishman I love talking and after leaving Blackpool I started to do some work as an after-dinner speaker. Not long afterwards, I spoke to a group of local business people and one of my themes was the changes that have taken place in football since "my day". I wondered aloud what it might have been like to play the beautiful game all nicely wrapped up in tights, gloves and even snoods (whatever they are). How things change!

I even spent some time working for a funeral director as a pall bearer although, predictably, I hated that role and soon gave it up. More recently, I have taken on a part time role driving a school bus, done charity work and still have property business interests. As for football, I'm becoming increasingly involved in the walking version which is great fun. Although I'd love to revive my old soccer schools in some form, at the moment I'm not sure I have the time or energy. Maybe in the future.

Lyn remains employed at the Trust to this day.

One negative aspect of retirement was my descent into depression. After leading such a full and active life, revelling in the company of many people, I struggled to adapt to a life in which, with Lyn at work and the kids at school, I was often alone for much of the day. I had too much time to brood about the past and worry about the future. I became deeply concerned about how I would cope moving forward financially. My family was still young and depended on me income-wise and I spent many sleepless nights as I mulled things over in my head.

Eventually, my anxiety levels were so great, I consulted my doctor and went for counselling. I refused, except for a brief period when I knew medication was the only way my condition could be stabilised, to take any pills and threw everything into the counselling. It proved very helpful and gradually I overcame the depression and am now back to my old self.

It was a frightening period of my life though and I'd encourage anyone who suffers with any form of mental health illness to do what I did and get help. It is not weak to admit you have mental health issues. Indeed, it is my view that it is a measure of a person's strength when they can acknowledge that they need help and then seek the assistance they need. Talking to someone neutral about my difficulties was a turning point and has helped me adapt to semi-retirement and enjoy life to the full again.

No one should suffer in silence.

Chapter 28

Fleetwood my second home, and reflections on family and career (May 2019)

As I wrote this chapter, it came as something of a shock when I realised that I have now lived in Fleetwood for over 23 years, just about a third of my life. It is now the place I call home and probably always will be.

In the early '90's I did contemplate moving back to Belfast. How different my life would have been had I done so. I wouldn't have married Lyn and there would have been no Thomas and Erin so thank God the Irish FA turned down my application for a job with them.

In total, I have lived in England, on and off, for 49 years. Not surprising then that I now consider myself to be half English, half Northern Irishman. My mother was English, all my four children were born in this country, so it has become natural for me to consider myself part English. I've even been known to support the England football team, although for many years that was probably because my 1982 World Cup omission still hurt so badly. Whatever the reason, I make no apologies for my "Englishness", although naturally I'll always be a proud Northern Irishman as well.

I have made many friends in Fleetwood and am comfortable here. The town has suffered enormously over the years with jobs disappearing at an alarming rate, but the town is full of good people and I would love for it to be rejuvenated by some inward investment to boost the local economy.

My wife Lyn is my rock. She is a superb mother and I like to think we have a very happy marriage. Our age difference means that Lyn still has some years to work before we can enjoy more home time together and I dream of one day buying us a luxurious camper van and the two of us travelling around the country together.

Thomas is now at College and as a talented singer and songwriter he has ambitions to make a career in the music industry. I will do everything to try and help him realise his dream but if talent has anything to do with it, he will not need any help from his old Dad.

Erin is now in secondary school and an aspiring model. She is a gorgeous kid and is already taking the first steps towards realising her ambitions in that direction.

Both Thomas and Erin are great kids. I love them dearly and I'm very proud of the people they are becoming. I have always viewed their complete lack of interest in football as a plus rather than a minus. They have their own ambitions and consequently will pursue their own dreams rather than trying to emulate my achievements in sport. Neither of them has a clue about my football career and I kind of like it that way. I hope, though, that through this book they do learn more about my life before them and realise with pride that I was once a footballer of some standing.

My elder children Leanna and Matthew remain a source of great pride to me and I see them on a regular basis. I love them dearly and both have formed great careers. Unlike Thomas and Erin, they knew me as a footballing Dad and whilst I still harbour some regrets about how my career and my divorce from their mother impacted them, they have turned out to be incredible people and I am very proud of them both. Their mother, Frances, deserves enormous credit for the people they have become.

I'm now in semi-retirement and one advantage is the space this gives me to pursue what I enjoy doing rather than what

I have to do. I still love joinery and building things and am constantly thinking of jobs I can carry out both on my family home and those properties which I rent out.

I'm also now able to reflect on my football career and focus more on the positives than the negatives. Despite not playing in the top-flight of English football and missing out on the 1982 World Cup finals, I had a great career which produced many special moments and memories. I loved playing for my country and will always treasure the goals I scored and the memory of playing with and against some of the best footballers of all time.

I adored my time at Bury (the first spell certainly) and Southend United, and whilst neither of my two stints with Blackpool worked out as I'd hoped, the club still means a lot to me. I was one of the first British players to move and play abroad (certainly in Greece) and it is a source of great pride to me that although the people who saw me play are a diminishing number, I am still greeted by fans of my ex clubs with enormous respect and adoration. That means everything to me. You play to entertain your clubs' fans and to earn their eternal respect is so special.

Whilst I admit to being a part-time England supporter, I'm now rapidly becoming a born-again Northern Ireland supporter. The events of 1982 hit me so badly that I had banished all thoughts of the national team from my mind. I'll be honest too and admit that the years after my career ended marked a growing disillusionment with the game. Not the playing or coaching of it, more the watching of it. Tackling has been virtually banished from the game and it often has an artificial look about it to me. 'Tiki taka' football is more ballet than football to my old eyes and over the years I watched the game less and less on TV and took virtually no notice of it in the press and media.

The appointment of my old mate Jimmy Nicholl as assistant manager for Northern Ireland reawakened my interest and Jimmy very kindly invited me to be his guest for one of the 2018 World Cup qualifiers.

It was wonderful - after an absence of approximately 35 years - to be back inside Windsor Park. The memories came flooding back; watching games there with my Daddy, playing for my country and living the dream.

I have since attended another international game there (see Chapter 29) and made a further trip in November to see the Euro 2020 qualifier versus the Netherlands, the team that provided the opposition for my greatest ever moment in football.

I love the honesty and work rate of the Northern Ireland team. They don't have the depth of quality players available to England but I maintain that the Northern Ireland players enjoy the experience more than their English counterparts and exhibit a greater pride and relish for the job.

I've even started taking more of an interest in my boyhood club, Spurs. It was incredible to watch their European Champions League semi-final victory over Ajax.

My old clubs have enjoyed mixed fortunes recently. Crusaders - the club where it all started for me - won two domestic cup trophies during season 2018/19 and Bury won promotion to League One, mirroring the achievement I enjoyed all those years ago with that lovely club (though of course what has happened since is terrible).

Southend United escaped relegation to League Two after a gripping last day of the season triumph over Sunderland. The match was televised live and I was overcome with the tension of it all as I willed my old club to do the business.

They won 2-1 with a dramatic late goal and the scenes at the end of the game reminded me of the celebrations when we won the Division Four title in the early '80's.

Blackpool missed out on the League One play-offs but the main aim that season of bringing about the conditions to end the fans boycott was achieved and I think that many fans - for now at least - cherish that more than the lure of Championship football.

My local club Fleetwood Town are established as a mid-table League One side which, considering their fan base, is a remarkable achievement.

I made many friends in the game and am particularly close to Wayne Harrison, Terry Pashley and Jimmy Nicholl. I always look forward to meeting up with them and love them as brothers. I am Chairman of the Blackpool FC Former Players Association and enjoy our periodic get togethers. I'm often invited back to events at Bury and Southend and I always feel privileged to see that so many people still warm to me and remember my exploits.

I see my siblings and my extended family whenever I can and remain very close to them all. I love them dearly and revel in the fact that I can now spend more time in their company.

Overall, I feel lucky to have lived the life I have had, enjoyed the career I had and raised the families that I so adore. There have been more ups than downs and I look forward to the future with excitement.

Chapter 29

Northern Ireland revisited [March 2019]

Whilst on the verge of finally finishing this book I realised that I still needed to research one or two details about my background in Northern Ireland. I also saw it as a chance to reward my friend, Paul Cambridge, who over the past 15 months has somehow made sense of my ramblings and helped me finish a project that means so much to me.

Paul had never visited Belfast before and as he and his lovely wife Judith are very close, she too accompanied us on our trip and ensured we kept to our promise that this was, at least in part, a working holiday.

This is our story.

Derek - Day 1

We set off from Fleetwood to catch the ferry to Belfast from Cairnryan in Scotland. This involved a car journey of about three hours which only proved problematical when on the outskirts of Stranraer I was so busy talking that I missed the signs for Cairnryan and ended up asking for directions. Completely out of character for me of course as I'm usually such a quiet and studious driver, and not a great start to fulfilling my promise to Paul and Judith that I knew where we were going like the back of my hand!

We enjoyed a couple of pints on the ferry. The prices were exorbitant so we would have needed a bank loan to enjoy a long session and therefore settled for a couple of scoops each.

My nephew, Michael, picked us up and after a few detours we arrived at my sister Isabella's house (Michael's mother) who had kindly agreed to let us stay over for three nights.

Michael is a great guy and he and Paul hit it off immediately and it was not long before I was the butt of their "I'm Derek Spence and I used to play with Bestie" jokes.

Paul - Day 1

Derek was kind enough to invite me to Belfast with him and also agreed to my wife Judith accompanying us. I hate being separated from her even for a few days so I was doubly grateful to him. I had long held an ambition to visit Northern Ireland so this was an invitation that I grabbed excitedly with both hands.

I had offered to help Derek complete this book in the early part of 2018 when, as a guest of chairman Steve Abbott, Derek accompanied us to a Thornton Cleveleys FC (TCFC) fixture away to Euxton Villa (I was/am General manager at TCFC). Unbeknown to Derek who, not surprisingly, had forgotten he had ever met me, I was no stranger to him as I had been a guest of our mutual friend, Paul Finnegan, when Derek acted as God Parent to Paul's son, Martyn, at his christening in Hambleton many years ago.

Our paths never crossed again until that fateful day in Euxton when I was soon reminded of this blokes' incredible capacity to talk. He literally never stopped. After grabbing a bacon butty just as we departed Thornton for the journey to Euxton, we were approaching Preston before he finally stopped talking long enough to take a bite of his butty, at which point he announced without any evident irony that the thing was stone fucking cold!

Since that day, as our work has progressed, I hope I am correct in thinking that we have grown to be good friends. I like Derek enormously. He is a crazy, fun guy and very kind and generous. I'm not nearly as much a people person as him and we therefore make unlikely buddies but I like and respect him enormously. And despite my constant teasing of him about his George Best stories, Derek is the most modest and unassuming of men.

We were staying in Belfast with his elder sister, Isabella, and were picked up at the port of Belfast by her son, Michael who drove us to his mother's house, but only after a quick stop off at the Crown and Shamrock pub and an even briefer detour to look at his childhood home. Consequently, we finally reached Isabella's beautiful home, in the lovely village of Templepatrick, approximately an hour later than envisaged.

Not a great start I thought nervously, first impressions being so important to relationships and all that, but I needn't have worried because Isabella was simply delighted to welcome us and was a wonderful and kindly host throughout the week. She is a terrific lady and Judith and I quickly warmed to her and intend to remain in touch with her. As for Michael, what a tremendous guy he is. Funny, generous and aimable as all the Spence clan proved to be.

Derek - Day 2

Up bright and early and after a quick breakfast we made our way to my childhood home at Serpentine Road where I showed my friends the places where I had played as a kid, the route of my paper round and we even stood outside the building which used to be my secondary school but which is now a school of music.

From there we moved onwards to the Crumlin Road and after learning that you could have a conducted tour of the famous old jail, we went in and thoroughly enjoyed a fascinating insight into the once notorious facility.

At about noon, we caught one of the red tour buses and were taken around Belfast, including the Shankhill and Falls Road areas where I had once worked as a young man. I loved every minute of it and the memories - good and bad - came flooding back. It had been a long time since I had set eyes on some of the places we travelled through and I realised, probably for the first time in years, just how much I loved, and sometimes missed, my city of birth.

After a brief walk on the Shankhill Road, we went back into the centre of Belfast to view the impressive Belfast City Hall and then on our way back to my car, we passed by the famous Europa Hotel, once the most bombed hotel in Europe. I made a mental note to ring my old Northern Ireland team-mate Bryan Hamilton who I knew was staying there before attending the international between Northern Ireland and Estonia the following day.

As a thank-you to Isabella for letting us stay with her, we intended to take her out in Templepatrick for a meal. Typically, Isabella wouldn't hear of it and generously insisted on paying. Spookily, the first person I saw as we entered the restaurant was Bryan Hamilton. I couldn't believe it. He was dining with some friends that I also knew and we chatted happily for such a long time that Isabella, Paul and Judith were on their main course by the time I reached their table.

After a couple of pints, Isabella and I made for home whilst Paul and Judith, showing far greater stamina, opted to stay for a few more scoops.

Paul - Day 2

A brilliant day from start to finish. As someone who had been an avid follower of news relating to the 'Troubles' throughout my childhood and beyond, I was fascinated by the tour of Crumlin Road jail and the bus ride through Belfast.

During the Crumlin Road jail tour, Derek soon became best pals with the guide and the only other tourist on the tour with us. Judith and I sniggered none too quietly as step by step, Snowball revealed his footballing identity only to be thwarted by the fact that as rugby lovers our companions knew nothing about football and consequently hadn't heard of him. George Best again saved the day though!

Incredibly, we discovered that the guide knew one of Derek's uncles who had worked at the jail in the '70's.

The Shankhill Road was of particular interest for me and once we embarked off the tour bus, I begged Derek to drive us back there so that I could take a stroll around.

With my recollections of its troubled past, albeit only via the television, I found it strangely liberating to simply walk into the Co-op shop and buy something as mundane as a packet of crisps and a diet coke. We also had a pint in the Rex Bar just off Snugville Street and, as usual, Derek was soon in conversation with a bunch of strangers at the bar. I swear I heard him mention George Best too.

His new pals had not only heard of Derek Spence the footballer but also remembered O'Hara's Bakery. They talked with some passion about the delights of their soda bread and other such products.

Back in the centre of Belfast there was time for another pint, this time in The Crown. Again, Derek made friends aplenty amongst the customers and staff. After a long wait for Judith and I at the pub exit, we finally dragged Derek out of the place so that we could immediately head for a Templepatrick restaurant and a meal in honour of Isabella.

Despite our protestations, Isabella refused to let us treat her and we enjoyed a sumptuous meal at her expense, fervently promising to return the favour when she is next in England.

Inexplicably, Derek bumped into Bryan Hamilton at the restaurant. What a lovely bloke he was. Even Isabella recognised him and visibly swooned as he visited our table for a brief chat whilst Derek continued to hold court with Bryan's companions.

A fantastic day ended with a few relaxing pints of lager before a sound sleep.

Derek - Day 3

I was due to meet a young lad called Stuart McKinley whose father had recently died. His dad was the Northern Ireland Kit man, and so Stuart wanted me to sign a book I featured in to dedicate it to his daddy's memory. He was trying to collect all the autographs of Ex Northern Ireland international players. I love doing this sort of thing and was eager to meet the young man so, as Paul was taking Judith to the Titanic exhibition in Glasgow, I agreed to meet him that lunchtime and then pick Paul and Judith up outside the Exhibition Centre for a trip to the Culloden Hotel where we were visiting Jimmy Nicholl and collecting some tickets off him for that nights' game versus Estonia.

Jimmy was in great form as usual. Paul follows Rangers and was eager to talk about Jimmy's spell as assistant manager there last season. Jimmy was full of stories and jokes, the highlight on this occasion being his reflections on attaining the illustrious status of Rangers interim manager and Northern Ireland manager simultaneously during the latter part of season 2018/19. The story went as follows:

"I was talking to my wife Sue and I asked her if, in even her wildest dreams, she had ever imagined me being manager of Rangers and assistant manager of my national side at the same time." Sue's reply, if Jimmy is to be believed went thus: "Jimmy love, you were never in my wildest dreams!" Classic.

He then entertained us with stories of how Manchester United fans had hated him when he first broke into their first team, the ending of his career with Northern Ireland, and many other hilarious anecdotes.

On the way back to Templepatrick, where we planned to have something to eat before heading for Windsor Park, Paul encouraged me to take a brief detour to the Crusaders ground. I took some selfies of me on the pitch and then had a brief drink in the social club where I scanned the pictures framed on the walls for sights of ex team-mates. I'll let Paul describe the rest of that particular visit for you.

The game at Windsor Park wasn't a classic by any means but Northern Ireland won 2-0 with goals from Niall McGinn and a penalty by skipper Steve Davis.

After the game I was invited to do a radio interview and was delighted to meet up with an old team-mate, John O'Neill.

A few pints in the Windsor Supporters Club, a midnight chippy meal and then the sweet relief of bed after a long but exhilarating day.

Paul - Day 3

Judith got to realise her ambition of visiting the Titanic exhibition whilst also pencilling in a future visit to the Game of Thrones site in Belfast.

I enjoyed the exhibition, but the highlight of the day for me was meeting ex Rangers star Jimmy Nicholl. He was brilliant company and I was thrilled to have a picture taken with him. It was lovely, as it had been the night before when we bumped into Bryan Hamilton, to witness Derek happily conversing with his old pal. They are obviously very close and I marvelled yet again at Derek's almost unique ability to maintain friendships with such a wide group of people who live long distances away from him and often lead such different lives. His footballing friends clearly love him as much as his non-footballing friends and it was clear that Derek was loving this trip and the opportunities it was providing to meet old and new acquaintances alike.

With this in mind I then persuaded Derek to visit his old haunt, Crusaders FC. I was delighted I did because he had a whale of a time. Apart from, that is, the fact that his photograph is conspicuous by its absence on the walls of the social club! Bestie's was there though and he had never even played for Crusaders!

Another player whose picture was prominent in the social club, was an ex team-mate of Derek's called Roy MacDonald. Roy is the elder brother of the late Queens Park Rangers and Northern Ireland centre half Alan McDonald. Derek estimated that he'd not seen or spoken to Roy since about 1969 but the gap in contact of approximately 50 years didn't faze Snowball in the least and with the help of an initially (and understandably) suspicious bar maid, he acquired Roy's mobile number and without hesitation or any thinking time, dialled the number.

To the open-mouthed amazement of Judith and I, Derek opened the conversation as follows:

"Alright Roy, I bet you can't guess who this is? Blond hair I had back then. Ha, bless you Roy, you guessed correctly. Yes, it's me, Derek Spence".

The conversation lasted 30 minutes and you'd never have guessed that half a century had passed since they last spoke. The call ended with Roy asking the bar maid to buy us all a pint on him. And the two of them agreeing to meet later in the year for a "proper catch up". That - my friends - is Derek Spence for you.

The game that night between Northern Ireland and Estonia was enjoyable and my first taste of Windsor Park and I loved it. Judith and Michael accompanied Derek and me and although Judith was knackered by the time the match ended, she sportingly joined in the after-match shenanigans

After Derek had completed an interview for Belfast radio, we went to the Windsor Supporters Bar and, typical of everyone I met in Belfast that week, the locals were incredibly friendly and welcoming. Everyone knew Derek of course and he was greeted like a returning hero.

Isabella had given me some home-made sausage rolls to eat during the game but in all the excitement I forgot they were in my pocket. She has clearly inherited her mother's talent for cooking as her status is already seemingly legendary, as proven by the grab of several desperate hands as I revealed the contents of my pocket. I have never seen sausage rolls wolfed down so quickly and with such relish.

The craic in the bar was wonderful and once again I became aware of just how special Belfast people are. I am so pleased for them that life in the province is now relatively peaceful and that they can live their lives without fear. That said, I nearly caused a national incident when in response to a question of "who is the best centre half in the world", I naively answered Vincent Kompany rather than what I was assured was the correct answer, Jonny Evans.

Having lost the sausage rolls and, much to Judith's disgust, yet another flat cap that I insist must be part of my football match garb, we went for a late-night chippy meal. What a day.

Day 4 - Paul

Sadly, it was time to go home. Isabella was a wonderful host and both Judith and I would love to stay in touch with her. Indeed, all the members of Derek's family that we met were incredibly nice. Lovely people all round.

I was also struck by the manner in which people working in pubs, shops and for tourist organisations represent their country and welcome visitors. It is no exaggeration to state that everyone we encountered was enormously warm and friendly and took great pride in learning how much we were enjoying our stay in their city. Businesses in the rest of Britain could learn a lot from their Northern Ireland cousins.

I fell in love with the place and almost felt more at ease there than I sometimes do in England. I can't wait to go back.

Derek's book is now complete but I hope that we remain friends and in touch. He is an incredible human being. His generosity to Judith and me whilst in Ulster was amazing. His book and his story deserves to be told. He was an admirable footballer and an even better human being. I hope you enjoy his story as much as I delighted in helping him tell it.

Day 4 - Derek

In the morning I took the opportunity to catch up with two of my sisters, Maureen and Diane, while Paul and Judith yarned the hours away with Isabella.

Michael again drove us to the ferry and I finally arrived home in Fleetwood at about midnight having enjoyed one of my best-ever trips home. Despite all the fun, we had captured the information we needed to complete this book. I was desperate to leave some sort of legacy of my career and life and I hope that you the readers feel I have achieved this. I hope too that my family enjoy it and I ask for their forgiveness if any of my recollections are inaccurate or different to theirs.

Thank you for reading my story. Love Derek.

Chapter 30

My all-time club team-mates XI - With a difference

John Forrest - Bury goalkeeper and farmer.

Steve Hoolican - Bury FC hardman who later became a publican.

Terry Pashley - Great pal and a team-mate at Bury and Blackpool. Excellent fullback

David Holt - Bury team-mate and my best man when I married Frances.

Paul Hart - Blackpool centre half who went on to play for clubs including Nottingham Forest, Leeds United and Sheffield Wednesday. A much-respected coach, Paul has also enjoyed a long career in management working for clubs such as Barnsley, Nottingham Forest, Queens Park Rangers, Crystal Palace and Swindon Town.

Alan Suddick - The King of Bloomfield Road.

George Hamstead - Winger for York City, Barnsley, Bury and Rochdale and served as reserve team coach at Bury after retiring from playing.

Bobby Collins - Ex Celtic, Everton and Leeds United ace and my team-mate at Oldham Athletic.

Keith Mercer - Southend United strike partner who also played with distinction for Watford and Blackpool.

Mickey Walsh - Blackpool idol who after a spell with Everton later played for FC Porto in Portugal and is now a football agent.

George Best - The greatest player of my lifetime and a Northern Ireland team-mate who I also played briefly with in Hong Kong.

Subs:

Keith Kennedy - Bury left back and brother of ex Liverpool and England defender Alan Kennedy.

Wayne Moffat Harrison - Another great friend with the best middle name ever. A team-mate at Blackpool who also played for clubs including Workington Town, Barrow and Carlisle United. Later, manager of Workington Town, Accrington Stanley and Bamber Bridge and Academy Director of Youth at Blackpool before moving to the USA to continue his coaching career.

Billy Ronson - Midfield dynamo for Blackpool who later played for Cardiff City before finishing his playing career in the USA.

George Wood - Blackpool and Scotland goalkeeper who also played for Everton, Arsenal, Crystal Palace, Cardiff City and Hereford United.

Derek Spence - You surely didn't expect me to leave myself out?

Manager: Allan Brown - My gaffer at both Bury and Blackpool and the man who got the best out of me and understood/believed in me the most.

Chapter 31

How Blackpool Got Its Club Back
By Steve Rowland

Sometimes in the weird and wonderful world of modern-day association football - with its riches, its wall-to-wall TV coverage and its players on multi-million pound contracts - it is worth remembering how all this started way back in the smoky haze of Victorian England's industrial heartland.

In those faraway days, the first properly constituted football clubs typically grew out of church youth clubs or factory socials. They were formed by earnest, civic minded men with paternalistic foresight who wanted to give young working-class lads with talent an opportunity to play the game competitively; and equally importantly, to give their peers and elders a chance to watch them and cheer them on, respite at the end of a hard week's labour, which typically included Saturday morning working - the reason why league games traditionally kick off at 3pm on Saturdays.

Then something transformative happened. As teams got more organised and the popularity of the league system grew, so did attendances and clubs quickly outgrew their parochial beginnings as church or works teams to become symbols of whole communities and a source of pride for the town or district in which they were based. Going to the game, meeting up with mates, supporting the team, all became a way of life, a social connection and a consuming passion for millions of our forefathers. Although much has changed in 150 years, that template was a sound one, for football is truly the national sport and still the most popular pastime in the UK today.

Blackpool FC pretty much followed the model outlined. Formed in 1887 by the men of St John's church, who felt that Blackpool should have a football club bearing the town's name, the team played in the Lancashire League for several years before being elected to the Football League in 1896. It shortly afterwards fixed on Bloomfield Road as its permanent base. That hallowed turf just inland from the promenade is still its home today, in the heart of the community.

After 30 years in the second tier, Blackpool won its first (and only) league title in 1930, finishing top of Division Two and finally securing elevation to the top flight of English football. Ironically it was World War II that indirectly gave the club its next big boost as talented footballers in the armed forces stationed in the town turned out for the club in the wartime regional league and many signed for Blackpool when the national league recommenced in 1946. The next 20 years can rightly be labelled Blackpool's glory years as a competitive first division force. They regularly finished in the top third of the table and contested three FA Cup finals, famously winning the trophy in 1953. It was this period that established Blackpool firmly in the footballing consciousness and affection of the nation and made many of its players - Matthews, Mortensen, Armfield among them - household names.

In the 1960s, with the abolition of the maximum wage and the arrival of more money into the professional game, a gulf began to open between the big city clubs and those with a smaller catchment. Blackpool found itself in the second category and its fortunes ebbed through the 1970's and 1980's as it dropped through the second and third and into the fourth division. At times it struggled to survive financially, while the likes Aldershot, Bradford PA,

Southport and Workington went to the wall for lack of investment and support, but survive it did, with the directors putting their hands in their pockets, on a loyal fan base of about 4,000 faithful supporters.

Perhaps one should always be mistrustful of the motives of people who buy football clubs for £1, as happened to Blackpool (when Owen Oyston purchased it in 1988) and to Bury (recently expelled from the EFL) in 2018. Of course, no one buys into a club with the intention of losing money, though as a business venture it's a gamble; and bank-rolling a club that is consistently losing money is an expensive hobby.

However, there was a paradigm shift in football's financial playing field in the 1990's with the creation of the Premier League. The amount of money being pumped in at the higher levels in terms of sponsorship sky-rocketed and suddenly the gains to be made out of a club playing at the level of Championship and above became seriously tempting to many who had not the slightest interest in football as a game or a way of life.

For most of the 1990s, Owen Oyston did little except keep the club ticking over in the lower divisions, though fans were grateful enough that he had saved Blackpool from potential extinction. However, since the millennium Blackpool's fortunes began to turn slowly on the rise again. Those fortunes were soon to take a quantum leap forward with the arrival in 2006 of Latvian businessman Valeri Belokon as a 20% shareholder. It was his involvement and additional funding in the stadium and the team which triggered the club's rise to the Championship and then the Premier League via the play-off final in May 2010.

Mr Belokon had promised to get the club there in five years. The transformation was achieved in four and to our enormous delight, Blackpool FC found itself back in the top-flight of English football again after an absence of 40 years. It was a Tangerine dream come true, and with Premier League revenues onstream, here surely was a chance to complete the renovation of the stadium, build a the fit-for-purpose training ground that was badly needed, and upgrade the operational infrastructure to make Blackpool a successful, modern football club in the heart of a reviving community. What could possibly go wrong? Well, where to start?

All of the above has been merely a preamble, a scene-setting to the real substance of this chapter, which is the story of the prolonged battle on several fronts since 2013 for the soul of Blackpool FC and how it eventually emerged from years of turmoil with a new owner, a re-energised fan base and a much-heralded fresh start in 2019.

The problems really began on the day the team in tangerine won that play-off final. Blackpool's promotion to the Premier League could and should have been just the start of a prolonged period in the top-flight, a carefully planned and sustainable future for the football club with the knock-on benefits which that would bring to the town, the community and the local economy. Bournemouth, Brighton and Burnley have all demonstrated that it is possible with the right philosophy and the right calibre of people. Sadly, Blackpool's majority owner and his family saw only pound signs and what was in it for them from winning the game that was dubbed "the richest prize in football", reputedly worth £90 million and more. Despite all of the pomp, ceremony and fine words from all quarters about what this elevation would mean for the club and the town, Blackpool lasted just a single season in the Premier League and manager Ian Holloway concluded famously that the house had been built on sand.

What nobody realised at the time was that on the club's accession to the top division, the Premier League had informed Owen Oyston in the summer of 2010 that he failed their fit and proper person's test - for reasons which are surely widely known and extensively documented elsewhere - and they instructed him to divest his majority share-holding and directorship of the football club. This he signally failed to do. Unfortunately, the Premier League didn't follow up to ensure his compliance and by the following May, with the team's relegation back to the EFL, it was no longer the Premier League's problem. Quite why the EFL didn't take the same view as the Premier League at the point when the club re-joined the Championship in 2011 has long been a point of contention for Blackpool fans.

It was strongly rumoured that during the Premier League season that Mr Belokon tried to persuade Mr Oyston to invest in strengthening the team to ensure its survival in the division. Allegedly he not only refused to do so but also apparently reneged on an agreement to increase Mr Belokon's shareholding in the club to 50%. Belokon had believed he was forging a partnership of equals with Mr Oyston. Events were to prove that his faith in the partnership was entirely misplaced.

Much of the behind-the-scenes fallout was not visible to fans of the club who had just enjoyed a magnificent season of football during which the team in tangerine had lit up the Premier League with its attacking style of play. Seasiders fans had been able to watch their heroes match themselves against the top sides in the country, winning away at Newcastle and Sunderland, beating Spurs at home, and doing the double over Liverpool. Blackpool had become most other supporters' second favourite team again. Relegation when it came, only confirmed in the final minute of the final game of the season, was on goal difference from

Birmingham City, both clubs finishing on 39 points - which in nine seasons out of ten would have been a big enough tally to ensure survival.

The first hint fans had that the financial rewards earned by the players on the pitch were not necessarily going to benefit the football club as expected came when Owen Oyston paid himself an £11 million director's emolument out of the monies accruing from Premier League status - this despite the fact the Premier League had declared him unfit to be a director. It was the largest single payment ever made by a club to one of its officials. Under Premier League rules, Blackpool as a relegated club was entitled to a series of parachute payments, payable over four seasons, to effectively compensate it for the drop from Premier League to Championship. The intention was to cushion a club with a Premier League squad and the contracts that implied from the falling revenue impact that a drop down to a lower division would have. The Premier League expected such parachute payments would be used to sustain the football club but there was nothing in writing that said this had to be the case, so the majority owner of Blackpool FC was free to apportion the millions coming into the football club as he saw fit - and what he saw fit (apart from that £11 million bonus to himself) was to loan millions more to various Oyston-owned enterprises on unsecured, open-ended terms.

Once supporters began to realise that Belokon was being side-lined and that most of the parachute payment millions were not going into sustaining the football club - that the stadium redevelopment would not be completed, that the promised training facility would never be built, that investment in the team was being pared back - then many started to voice concerns about the disposition of monies and what they termed the squandering of the legacy. Some, the writer of this chapter included, sought collective action by the fan base to try and bring the pressure of public opinion to bear on the owners. Dissatisfied that the officially recognised Blackpool Supporters' Association was not representing our concerns, we formed the Seasiders' Independent Supporters Association in 2013 and a year later voted to recast itself formally as a supporters' trust in line with the model developed by Supporters Direct and approved by the Minister of Sport.

Blackpool Supporters' Trust (BST) quickly became the largest fans' organisation in the history of the football club with over 2,000 paid-up members (a very high percentage given the size of the fan base). With the tagline 'putting football first' to flag up our belief that the Oystons were not doing so, BST set its stall out as follows: "We believe that a football club belongs first and foremost to the community of its supporters. Chairmen and directors come and go but without supporters (the ongoing heart and soul of the club), there would be no Blackpool Football Club. So the Supporters' Trust was formed, not as a protest group but as a positive force for change in the way that Blackpool FC is run, dedicated to giving the football club back to the community." As a legally constituted and independent community benefit society, open and affordable to all fans, and run on transparent and democratic lines, BST sought - and still does - to represent the best interests of fans and club alike and to hold the owners of the club (whoever they might be) to account in the interests of the community. For we believe that football clubs are social enterprises, rooted in that tradition outlined at the beginning of this chapter, and not just businesses to be run (for better or frequently for worse) by whoever happens to own the majority shareholding, usually with an eye to the main chance.

We initially sought dialogue with the owner and the chairman of Blackpool FC, to have our concerns formally tabled and addressed. They simply refused to recognise BST or to talk with our representatives. At the same time a war of words was developing on online message boards and via social media. Individual supporters were quite often very stinging in their condemnation of the actions of the Oystons and unfortunately the chairman of the club goaded supporters in turn. The chairman was fined and disciplined by the FA for one outburst but worse was to follow when the Oystons started legal proceedings against individual supporters for comments made on social media, including allegations that the Oystons were asset-stripping the football club; (allegations that a High Court judge eventually deemed to be true - but that comes later).

If there is one thing guaranteed to turn a set of football supporters against the owners of their club, it is when the owners start taking legal action against fans. It's anathema as far as the fan base is concerned. In Blackpool's case, it wasn't just one or even two rash and outspoken supporters. The Oystons instigated the threat of litigation against 15 people in all, among them pensioners and the then chairman of BST, the latter for repeating allegations of asset-stripping that had been voiced in the press.

Blackpool began the 2014-15 Championship season with only eight professional players on its books. It was a shambles of a start that didn't get any better. Anti-Oyston banners, chants and protests became frequent at games throughout the season while the chairman continued to insist that all was well, claimed that Blackpool was the envy of the football league and invited fans to judge him come May. The team was bottom of the league through the whole campaign and finished with a record low points total. The season culminated in a huge protest march along Bloomfield Road to the ground by thousands of angry fans prior to the last home game - the Judgement Day that the

Oystons had called on themselves - and later that afternoon a pitch invasion saw the game against Huddersfield abandoned as Blackpool were relegated back to the third tier.

The following season commenced with an 'ethical boycott' in place, the threat of more legal action by the owners against fans and another abysmal season on the field. The ethical boycott was at minimum a withholding from the club (i.e. the Oystons' coffers as fans saw it) of all monies apart from the price of a match-day ticket for those who continued to follow the team. This line quickly hardened into 'not a penny more' for thousands of erstwhile loyal supporters. It was a principled decision taken by the majority of Blackpool fans and it was to continue for the next three seasons, a concerted action without parallel in English football. Literally thousands of ardent Blackpool supporters vowed never to enter Bloomfield Road again or give the club a penny of their money while the Oystons remained in control - even if it meant they would never watch the team they loved again. The strength of feeling cannot be overstated. Attendances dropped by three-quarters.

Blackpool suffered a second successive relegation in 2016, back into the bottom division of the Football League; that's top-flight to bottom in six years - a calamitous fall, evidence of the dire under-investment in the club (despite it being supposedly 'cash-rich') and proof for those who believed this was cynical intention rather than incompetence on behalf of the owners of what became termed 'managed decline'. Inevitably, May 2016 saw a repeat of judgement day. JD Two was bigger and louder than the previous end-of-season protest as thousands of boycotting fans wearing 'Oyston Out' scarves and carrying banners marched from the centre of town along the promenade to the stadium to hold a protest rally. There were many more supporters who stayed outside the ground than there were inside it that day.

And so it continued. When supporters wanted to give club hero Brett Ormerod a testimonial game, BST arranged for the match to be played not at Bloomfield Road but at nearby AFC Fylde. And for those who wanted to show their allegiance to the concept of supporting Blackpool even though as fans 'in exile', supporters sourced an 'alternative' Blackpool shirt (via Adidas) that sold very well without a penny going to the Oystons, and raised several thousand pounds for charity in the process.

Although Bloomfield Road was eerily empty for the season in the bottom division, with away supporters frequently outnumbering home fans, the team under manager Gary Bowyer actually did well enough to reach the play-offs. Many were expecting that this would precipitate a bit of a crisis for Blackpool's boycotting thousands. We had taken 35,000 to Wembley in 2010. Would the not-a-penny-more resolve fold in the face of another Wembley visit? Not a bit of it. One half of Wembley stadium was nearly empty that day as a mere 5,000 tickets were sold for the Blackpool end and surely no-one in the country with a modicum of interest in football could miss the point that was being made. Meanwhile 250 miles further north, every pub and club in the town was rammed with Blackpool fans watching the final on TV, willing their team to win, having sacrificed the chance to be at the game on a point of principle. I should have mentioned that weeks prior to that the home season had concluded with the now traditional judgement day march, JD Three being the biggest and angriest, swelled by the ranks of sympathetic Leyton Orient supporters, no strangers themselves to the damage that 'rogue' owners could visit upon the football clubs under their charge.

All through these years of boycott, exile and protest, Blackpool Supporters' Trust was working not only for regime change at Bloomfield Road but was looking to broaden the campaign into one for reform of football governance as a whole, to try and persuade the football authorities to do more to protect the interests of the most important stakeholders in the game - the fans - rather than just looking after the shareholders. After all, without fans, there would be no football clubs. It was an uphill task. Regular appeals were made to the EFL and the FA. Detailed complaints were lodged with the Independent Football Ombudsman. The FA said the responsibility lay with the EFL as a competition organiser. The EFL said governance was an FA responsibility and anyway the Oystons had not contravened any EFL rules. The team, newly promoted back to the third tier (now called League One), continued to play in a three-quarters empty Bloomfield Road.

Meanwhile, one man was about to act where the football authorities wouldn't or couldn't and was about to achieve what the boycotting fans on our own could never bring about. Valeri Belokon was building a civil prosecution under the Companies Act and was going to take Owen and Karl Oyston and their Blackpool FC holding company to the High Court on the grounds of unfair prejudice relating back to their actions in 2010 in effectively side-lining his involvement and reneging on the partnership deal. Belokon retained one of the best legal teams in the country and, although the judicial wheels rolled slowly through 2017 and 2018 in Manchester and London's High Court, Mr Justice Marcus Smith eventually ruled that the Oystons had illegitimately stripped the assets of Blackpool FC, had acted with prejudice against Mr Belokon and his interests and in a forensic 167 page judgement confirmed what most of us had believed all along. In an historic ruling at the end of

2017 he ordered that the Oystons should recompense Mr Belokon to the tune of £31 million (plus costs).

Those of us in court for the hearing and the judgement still count it as among the best of away days! That judgement was a game-changer. We knew then that sooner or later, somehow we would see an Oyston-free Blackpool FC and would be able to return to not only supporting but actively watching the Seasiders again; and it is our belief that the judge was mindful throughout the whole process of the impact the turmoil at Blackpool FC was having on its community of fans. He offered Mr Belokon the option of a court-appointed receiver for the football club at an early stage but that was declined as Mr Belokon hoped to negotiate a reasonable settlement with the Oystons.

We half expected that Owen Oyston would offer to sell Blackpool FC to Mr Belokon in part mitigation of the £31 million award, but he didn't. Instead he adopted delaying tactics. He put the club up for sale but wouldn't entertain any offers. He tried to appeal the judgement without success and then he just prevaricated for months, claiming he was always on the point of securing a massive loan that would enable him to pay off the £31 million and retain control of Blackpool FC, whose gates and revenue streams were now so low that it was losing several million pounds per season. No one could fathom the sheer illogicality of Oyston's tactics as he defaulted time and again on rescheduled payment dates and as the interest he would have to pay racked up additional thousands per week. This impasse went on for a further year until Mr Belokon finally lost all patience and went back to the High Court to request that a receiver be appointed.

Thus it was that in February 2019, 30 years after he bought it for £1, six years after the birth of SISA, five years after the formation of Blackpool Supporters' Trust, four years after the wholesale boycott began to take effect and two years after legal proceedings commenced, that the Oyston family's hands were finally and for good prised off Blackpool Football Club.

It took a few weeks for the court appointed receiver to secure the bank accounts, because even then the departing owners were not going easily, and then we could plan our glorious home-coming parade for Saturday March 9th. Thousands of fans who had been boycotting for years (and some who hadn't - but we're magnanimous in victory) gathered once again on a beautifully sunny day on Blackpool promenade and paraded in a sea of tangerine flags, alternative shirts and Blackpool Are Back scarves along the old judgement day route to Bloomfield Road which was packed to the rafters for the first time in nearly a decade. It was a spine-tingling occasion, easily as emotional as that day when we won promotion to the Premier League and thought we'd entered the dreamland (only to find it turned into a nightmare).

In the close season, the receiver pushed on with the sale of the football club. We believe we are very fortunate that it has been bought by a wealthy life-long fan, someone who says he felt it almost a civic duty to step in and rescue this historic club, who recognises the immense importance it has in the life of the supporters and the town and who regards himself as a custodian of the social enterprise that is Blackpool FC. It will take time for the rebuilding of the infrastructure after years of neglect (for want of a better word), time to reconnect the fan base with the team of players currently wearing the famous tangerine shirt and time to take Blackpool onwards and upwards as a vibrant and sustainable modern football club in the heart of a reviving community - everything we hoped was on the agenda but didn't materialise a stormy decade ago. This time though, we dare to dream that it will happen and will do all we can as involved supporters to help it come to pass. Having made the sacrifices and fought the battles that we have in the last few years, it would be unthinkable that we should fail to build a better and brighter future for Blackpool Football Club to the lasting benefit of the community and the town.